"If you need a slow-living guide—a guide out of the crush of noise and the exhausting speed of life—Jodi Grubbs is a gentle sage who has faced suffering and heartbreak. She shows us the road less traveled—into a far more meaningful life."

Ann Voskamp, author of *One Thousand Gifts* and *The Broken Way*

"In a culture that overvalues hustle and undervalues wholeness, finding spaces that honor our God-given humanity can be a challenge. Yet in *Live Slowly*, Jodi Grubbs compassionately and authentically invites us to a way of being that roots us in our truest identity as God's beloved. This book is a love letter to anyone feeling overwhelmed, out of alignment, and tired of pushing beyond their limits. I'm deeply grateful for Jodi's words."

Aundi Kolber, licensed professional counselor and author of *Try Softer*

"Jodi Grubbs brings a unique perspective on the challenge of hurry that we face. Growing up in a less hurried culture and living as an adult in our more hurried one has borne the fruit of practical insight and wise guidance. I encourage you to read this book if you're seeking to follow the less hurried way of Jesus. You'll find a lot of help here!"

Alan Fadling, president of Unhurried Living Inc. and author of *A Non-Anxious Life*

"Some books come to us exactly when we need them. *Live Slowly* will undoubtedly be a timely gift for those who find themselves worn out by the hurried pace of contemporary life. Jodi Grubbs is an experienced guide to the sacred geography of slow living. Filled with Jodi's deeply personal stories, wise words from the many Christians she has read and befriended, and tangible practices for slowing down, this book is a lifesaver. I recommend it for all who have felt their exhausted heads slipping beneath the waves of hurry, hustle, and stress."

Christie Purifoy, author of *Placemaker* and *Garden Maker*

"The beach has long been a place of rest and refreshment. Sand, palm trees, driftwood, crashing waves, and flip-flops are all part of my regular rhythm of life. Jodi's island theme is the perfect setting for intentional soul care amid pressing cultural dynamics. I trust Jodi because she has lived a with-God life smack in the middle of unimaginable loss. She is uniquely capable of journeying with us as we learn to slow to the pace of an ocean wave. Read this book and trust that you have a reliable friend accompanying you on your journey toward slowness of heart, soul, and mind."

Gem Fadling, founder of Unhurried Living Inc. and author of *Hold That Thought*

"*Live Slowly* is a beautifully written and much-needed book. Through soft and honest words, Jodi Grubbs invites us to slow down, exhale, and remember the unending love and kindness of God. Page after page, you'll feel the weight lifted off your shoulders as your eyes are refocused on the One who invites us to walk with him."

Tanner Olson, author and poet

"I didn't think I needed permission to live slowly. But in reading these beautiful, inviting, life-giving words by Jodi Grubbs, I felt a weight I didn't know I was bearing slowly lift. Read this book and you will feel it too."

Karen Swallow Prior, author of *The Evangelical Imagination: How Stories, Images, and Metaphors Created a Culture in Crisis*

"*Live Slowly* offers readers hope that it is possible to live an unhurried life in our fast-paced world. It tenderly grants us permission to intentionally shift toward a life that God intended for us at the beginning of time—one that is slower, more meaningful, and filled with fellowship with God and others. This book encourages us to savor each moment, linger longer, listen attentively, and be fully present. With vivid imagery, Jodi Grubbs transports us to island living and beckons us to create our own 'Island in the City.' *Live Slowly* is a beautifully written gift our hurried souls have longed for."

Natasha Smith, author of *Can You Just Sit With Me? Healthy Grieving for the Losses of Life*

"In Proverbs we're told that 'the purposes of a person's heart are deep waters, but one who has insight draws them out.' In *Live Slowly*, Jodi Grubbs takes us on a deep dive into the depths of our hearts to insightfully and gently surface the purposes of our fast-paced existence. This guided deep dive will breathe life into your exhausted soul, as it did mine. You will receive truth, compassion, hope, and the practical, spiritual tools you will need to find your soul rest in Jesus."

Kenny Latimore, pastor of Garner Advent Christian Church

"The deeper I got into this book, the more my shoulders dropped and the deeper I exhaled. Jodi Grubbs has written one long permission slip that you were not made for hurry and production, chased by impossible expectations; you were made to live as a beloved child. She teaches that the more you learn to keep in step with the pace God has given you, the more you are able to love expansively. Jodi practices what she preaches. Just like her book, whenever you're in her presence, your shoulders drop and you exhale slowly, knowing she has plenty of time to enjoy your company. She's her Abba's daughter."

Summer Joy Gross, author of *The Emmanuel Promise: Discover the Security of a Life Held by God*

"*Live Slowly* is a refreshingly practical and unassuming guide to the contemplative life. Jodi Grubbs walks the reader by the hand to the cozy armchair, the wide-open field, the place of stillness where God can be heard over the cacophony of our modern world. Every line brims with care and intention; the 'slow living shifts' and suggested rhythms and practices found in these pages are invaluable tools for the journey. *Live Slowly* is a gift for anyone longing for a different pace but struggling to slow down."

Taylor Leonhardt, singer-songwriter

"Jodi Grubbs is a woman after my own heart, offering a gentle but steady drumbeat for anyone desperate for a saner, slower, less hustle-y way of living. And now she's put all her best advice and shimmering stories into one book. *Live Slowly* is a valuable resource for anyone seeking to live a life of deeper meaning, connection, and spiritual fulfillment. Whether you're overwhelmed by a busy schedule or simply yearning for a more intentional way of living, this book offers a road map to help you find your rhythm—and exhale in God's grace."

Jennifer Dukes Lee, author of *Growing Slow* and *It's All Under Control*

Jodi H.
Grubbs

live
slowly

A Gentle
Invitation
to Exhale

ivp

An imprint of InterVarsity Press
Downers Grove, Illinois

InterVarsity Press
P.O. Box 1400 | Downers Grove, IL 60515-1426
ivpress.com | email@ivpress.com

InterVarsity Press® is the publishing division of InterVarsity Christian Fellowship/USA®. For more information, visit intervarsity.org.

Scripture quotations marked MSG are taken from The Message, copyright © 1993, 2002, 2018 by Eugene H. Peterson. Used by permission of NavPress. All rights reserved. Represented by Tyndale House Publishers.

While any stories in this book are true, some names and identifying information may have been changed to protect the privacy of individuals.

Published in association with the Books & Such Literary Management, 52 Mission Circle, Suite 122, PMB 170, Santa Rosa, CA 95409-5370, www.booksandsuch.com.

Interior image credits: Hand drawn seafood illustration ©Yevheniia via Canva.com
  coconut cocktail hand drawn illustration ©ilonarepkina via Canva.com
  milk jug pitcher ©Victoria Sergeeva via Canva.com
  lemon slice illustration ©helenreveur via Canva.com
  sand bucket with shovel illustration ©Invisual Studio via Canva.com

The publisher cannot verify the accuracy or functionality of website URLs used in this book beyond the date of publication.

Cover design: David Fassett
Interior design: Daniel van Loon
Cover images: Getty Images: © Surasak Suwanmake / Moment, © Karl Hendon / Moment,
        © Yifei Fang / Moment

ISBN 978-1-5140-0708-2 (print) | ISBN 978-1-5140- 0709-9 (digital)

Printed in the United States of America ⬦

Library of Congress Cataloging-in-Publication Data
A catalog record for this book is available from the Library of Congress.

31 30 29 28 27 26 25 24 | 12 11 10 9 8 7 6 5 4 3 2 1

To

Dean and Lili,

the loves of my life.

You are the avocado to my toast.

Thank you both (and the cats of course)

for being my biggest fans!

Contents

A Return to Everyday Island Living

*My story is important not because it is mine, God knows,
but because if I tell it anything like right, the chances are
you will recognize that in many ways it is also yours.*

FREDERICK BUECHNER

THIS BOOK COMES FROM A PLACE of deep searching, of being pulled between two cultures. Not just geographically, but socially and culturally. Torn between a hustle culture that was foreign but seemed inevitable while also trying to remember my roots from a culture of slow and steady.

I was born and raised on Bonaire, a small Dutch island in the Netherlands Antilles, which is part of the southern Caribbean. My father worked in finance for Trans World Radio, a global Christian media organization.

What I did not know when I left the island at age sixteen was that I would wrestle with these two cultures many times over the next three decades. One would try to pull me into the land of hurry—of never enough and the fear of missing out, focused on striving, people pleasing to fit in, and filling my calendar with yeses that were not really thought through. I did not know that the grounding and lifesaving culture that gave me breath in my formative years would be one I would struggle to hold on to, like fine beach sand slipping through my fingers.

Despite being a former island girl, used to living on what we have all heard as "island time," I've had my share of long seasons of exhaustion, hustling, and people pleasing. As you hold this book in your hands, I want you to know that you are not alone, that you have it in you to shift toward a more sustainable pace, to recover your precious life and stay there.

I'm here to walk this path with you, showing you what I've both learned and then unlearned. Helping you—so you don't have to repeat my mistakes. Giving you life-giving concepts, spiritual disciplines, slow living practices, and easy rhythms that I knew from my island life, but somehow forgot.

Come. Slow down and breathe easily and deeply again! Maybe you were never even meant to be moving through life as fast as you have been. Longing to linger with God and connect to others is normal. The need you feel to stop and finally catch your breath is healthy and possible. While I can't offer you a literal stretch of sandy beach to walk on, I can come alongside you as a fellow sojourner and soul nourisher.

Are you anticipating pushback from other people in your life who don't understand your deep personal need to exhale? Are you afraid of looking weak or lazy? Are you wondering if slowing down might mean you are actually letting others down? Or maybe like me, do you have a fear of missing out?

If so, I invite you to shift:

From exhausted to refreshed and settled.
From hurry and hustle to gentle contemplation.

From lonely to enjoying barefoot hospitality.
From feeling not seen to truly being held.

Perhaps you simply need someone to affirm you as you take your next steps to identifying and advocating for your unique pace, practicing soul care, finding your people, and simplifying your faith through a fresh, ongoing friendship with God. Come linger. You'll find solidarity in the stillness. You'll find a deeper sense of community with your people and with the Trinity. You'll thrive from a place of rest as you trust that you are being held.

I wish I could tell you that I have done things perfectly— however, I have not. And that is okay. We keep learning. It was my doctor who had to tell me that my people pleasing, over-scheduling, and church volunteering was making me exhausted and constantly stressed. I didn't want to believe her until I started to see the trail of a broken life I was leaving in my wake.

These broken pieces had me sometimes snapping at my family to help prepare for yet another small group meeting. It meant being housebound many Halloween nights because I kept getting pneumonia and bronchitis, year after year, as I pushed my body beyond its limits each autumn. It looked like no white space on my paper calendar where healthy pauses should have been. Our bank account frayed trying to keep up with the Joneses each season, especially at the holidays.

If you see yourself in any of these life-draining scenes, you're in the right place. And you don't have to feel embarrassed or dis-couraged. Our culture dictates a lot of spoken and unspoken ex-pectations. I didn't realize that letting others down to catch my own breath was also self-care.

In a hustle culture like the one we've been in for so long, we don't know what we don't know. Until we do. Or, in my case, until I remem-

I didn't realize that letting others down to catch my own breath was also self-care.

bered my roots again. After what seemed like a hurricane of stormy life events and insecure decisions in the last three decades, my soul started longing to take in another version of that salty island air that I once knew so intimately. I wanted to spend more quality time with my people. I wanted the space to say yes to opportunities that could not be squeezed into an already-packed month. I wanted to live unhurried, leaning in to learn more about myself, God, and others, but in new ways. I love that John Ortberg wrote Dallas Willard's wise words on a piece of paper that still hangs above his office door. John's note says, "Arrange your days so that you experience total contentment, joy, and confidence in your everyday life with God."

As I started implementing the things I share in this slow living guide, it was almost as if I started feeling, tasting, and smelling that familiar salty air wrapping me in deep soul care, welcoming me back to a slower, more intentional way of life. By keeping my soul on island time while living in the city, I have relearned how to thrive from a place of rest, anchor into deep community, and come to believe that I am being held through these hard and busy seasons of life.

Coming home to our little "island in the city" has healed my exhausted heart in the most profound ways in these last five years. Salty air soul care is anchoring me back in. I know I belong here—not just in this physical location, a 1950s bungalow off Main Street in our little North Carolina town. I belong in this lifestyle, shifted to fit my dreams, my energy level, my health, and my family's bandwidth. It's more in line with the way God made me. And I want this for you too.

We're in this together. You're not doing this by yourself. I am here to gently and repeatedly remind you that this shift to slow living is a journey and a lifestyle, not a destination or latest craze. Like a brilliant piece of sea glass, remade after a rough and lengthy tumbling, we have a chance to remake our lives, our pace, and our future—one small, steady shift at a time. As J. R. R. Tolkien said, "Little by little, one travels far."

The words that best describe **SLOW** all have a contemplative stance.

S = *shift*: not an abrupt stop, but a slowing down like gears on a bike; a pivot

L = *linger*: this is a call to pause, to take your time and be present

O = *open hands*: expectant and yet vulnerable; asking God, "What now?"

W = *watchful*: observe; being alert in watching out for that pull back to hurry

Slow Living Shift
Introduction

Have you ever been so tired that you didn't have the energy to find your way to that cool drink or comfortable chair on your own? You needed someone to take you there. My offering to you is a curated selection of eighteen slow living concepts that will help you shift to slower living. These ideas will be foundational and life-giving as you set your new pace in motion.

> "Stand at the crossroads, and look; ask for the ancient paths, ask where the good way is, and walk in it, and you will find rest for your souls" (Jeremiah 6:16 NIV).

Visualize one of those signposts you might see in a beach town. There are various shapes and sizes of driftwood secured on it, all with different destinations painted on those wooden pieces. Each piece of driftwood is pointing in a different direction. Just like taking one trip at a time, slow living shifts are best learned one at a time, where you can be fully present to take it all in.

Each **Slow Living Shift** in this book is identified by a welcoming palm tree symbol. Soon these concepts will feel as comfortable as your favorite pair of flip-flops. Let them be part of the daily nourishment you need on your new journey toward slower living. None is more important than another. You can learn about them one by one in each chapter as you read sequentially, or wait till you see one you like and try it.

I see your weariness. It's real. And it's my delight to walk you through gentle rhythms that are tried and true as well as relevant concepts that might be new. I want you to be a healthier, rested version of your best self as you find your unique way to be in the world—walking into community with God and others. I already see the empowered person you are becoming as you stand up for yourself and those you love, paving the way to a new sustainable pace.

"Stand at the crossroads, and look; ask for the ancient paths, ask where the good way is, and walk in it, and you will find rest for your souls."
JEREMIAH 6:16 NIV

If you long for a different pace for your days with more time for the things that mean the most to you, this is your personal invitation to grab on to my hand, pause and take a deep exhale, right where you are. Here's to inhaling the salty air as we steady our stride, shift our direction, and continue to walk out this journey together! As this season ends, I know you will find your way again and enjoy a bit of everyday island living right where you are. You are not alone.

PART ONE

A Desperate Need to Exhale

Live in the sunshine,
swim in the sea,
drink the wild air . . .

RALPH WALDO EMERSON

1

When Sea Breeze and Road Rage Collide

The cost of a thing is the amount of life which is required to be exchanged for it.

Henry David Thoreau

It was early on a summer morning, and I was barely awake. Sunrise was imminent. I was twenty-seven years old and holding tight to my fresh dream of moving to Murrells Inlet, a small South Carolina coastal town we had just returned from visiting. Little did I know how many of my dreams would vanish that day. I ran out of our bedroom to call 911 at my husband Brian's request. A kind voice answered at the other end, but at the sound of Brian's body crashing onto the floor, I left the phone dangling. I quickly retraced my steps to find Brian dying. His aorta had ruptured, and he bled to death in less than two minutes, with me by his side.

The sound of breath, of life, leaving his body was louder than I had expected. It was a literal soft whooshing sound. The closest thing I had ever experienced was when I was fifteen. A thirty-foot whale shark surfaced right next to where I drifted with my friend in a small sailboat. Both situations were terrifying and yet beautiful in inexplicable ways. Both caught me by surprise and formed a lump in my throat. But that morning, as I felt bewilderment, fear, and disbelief, I wondered if I was caught up in a nightmare.

Two years prior, on a summer afternoon, coming around the bend in the road on Interstate 85 near Atlanta, Brian was riding as a passenger in a work truck that inadvertently found itself in the middle of a road rage incident. Brian had nowhere to go; he was crushed under a semi truck in this most horrific accident. Life came to a standstill that day. Due to the actions of strangers, Brian hovered between life and death. That day turned into nine months in the hospital, four of them in a shock-trauma ICU where my island heart saw human suffering so tragic it remains hard to explain.

Thirty-three surgeries and almost two million dollars in medical bills later, Brian eventually made a full recovery. We were settling into our own happy version of a slow and settled life in our quaint Georgia town—only to have those dreams vaporized that summer morning when Brian unexpectedly died. His aorta ruptured due to the infection and trauma near the site of his tracheostomy from two years earlier.

Maybe it's a good thing we don't write our own stories.

My grieving was intense that season. It was layered from the trauma my mind and body went through during the months when Brian had so many close calls in the hospital. It feels unbearable when you watch someone endure agony, and you can't prevent their pain and suffering.

Maybe it's a good thing we don't write our own stories. Sure, we make decisions, we plot a course, and go full steam ahead with our hopes and dreams—but we don't actually write our story.

God does. Our story fits into his Story and is woven in with other stories so big it's hard to imagine we are part of them. And yet we are. I still don't know the "why" of my story. I suppose I don't have to. You, too, may have a story that has left you wondering why. Maybe the unthinkable has happened to you. Maybe, what you had hoped *would* happen didn't.

Looking back as an adult, it sometimes seemed that my years as an island child were like living in the Garden of Eden. Such a beautiful, pristine dot in the world—a theology of slow living in the making. After college, I thought I would bring my peaceful, slow-paced island life with me as I got married and moved to Georgia. Sixteen years of slow island living in my formative years laid the groundwork for my life; but as often happens, a shattering life moment, like a crashing wave, threatened to tear apart the life I knew.

To Feel or Not to Feel

For so many years after this double tragedy of Brian's accident and later death, my biggest fear of slowing down came because I knew I'd need to sit with the hard stuff. I knew that I might not get answers. But mostly, I didn't want to *feel* the feelings. Those things I refused to think about, relive, question why, or deal with. There was a loneliness in knowing that many people around me either couldn't fathom my experiences or had moved on from them. My heart could bear reliving trauma only so much—which is probably why I put off important therapy for eighteen years after that.

There looms this underlying fright and agitation in not wanting to pause, not wanting to let time and stillness carve out things you cannot name. It's a universal fear because we all know that control very often slips out of our hands like sand. On her Instagram, Tutu Mora writes, "Feeling the need to be busy all the time is a trauma response and fear-based distraction from what you'd be forced to acknowledge and feel if you slowed down."

For most of us it's easier to plan a busy weekend of constant social obligations than it is to make space to talk to our partner or our parents about that looming difficult thing. We might even tackle a big project so we can avoid dealing with siblings bickering or teenagers' attitudes. However, not wanting to face God and admit that we aren't sure if we even trust him—even though we are leading the women's Bible study at church, serving on a mission board, or volunteering at the soup kitchen—is a whole 'nother thing, as we say here in the South.

Our bodies and our minds were not meant to keep up this wild pace. What we desperately need is a shift, a collective exhale as we find our way again.

If you're like me, there are times when it's easier to keep busy: head down, putting one foot in front of another. Until we can't. When we burn out from the busyness and we are forced to stop, this is our invitation to take inventory of all the unsaid, the undone, the unobserved. This divine pause creates time to reflect and gives us the opportunity to shift. It opens up a whole new world if we only let it. Our bodies and our minds were not meant to keep up this wild pace. What we desperately need is a shift, a collective exhale as we find our way again.

After Brian's death, I started an internal journey, wrestling with trusting the God I had known my whole life. I would have to unlearn some things in the years ahead and begin anew to believe that I was truly held by God. The same God who breathed life into Adam when he formed him from dirt. The same God who walked the garden with Adam and Eve in the cool of the day.

The Bible says: "And the dust returns to the earth as it was, and the breath returns to God who gave it" (Ecclesiastes 12:7 NRSV). The name God reveals for himself in Exodus, "I AM WHO I AM," is spelled YHWH in Hebrew. When I pronounce it, it only comes out as a breath, a soft whooshing sound.

Breath. Life. Death. I am in awe.

Slow Living Shift
Exhaling

Shifting the way we do things, the direction we are going in, and the way we are trying to hold it all together is imperative when intentionally slowing down. We will find freedom in naming our pain, our stories, and what we need. Do you need to shift your direction in order to turn a fresh page? Do you need to exhale, pausing to catch your breath from the last few years? We simply cannot keep holding our breath, wondering where the next disappointment or demand will come from. When we do, we are being robbed of time in our right-now, precious life.

Have you ever noticed that sometimes God seems really slow? The day my pastor, Kenny, asked that question from the pulpit, there was a sweeping wave of agreement in the nods, weary smiles, and sighs of our little congregation. As I sat there in the old wooden pew, looking up at the brass lanterns hanging high above me, I had one of those slow-drifting-out-to-sea moments. It was Advent. As I pondered Pastor Kenny's words, I saw the paradox. The golden glow lit up the space where the tiny crosses were set in our old church lights hanging from the high rafters. With little beacons of hope shining through, I felt an exhale, a relaxing of my shoulders. And yet, the stark reality of the hustle and the pain in the world was right outside our doors, a busy world we no doubt would all immerse ourselves in throughout that Advent season.

But for a while now, I have sensed a shift beginning—a collective pushing back on the social norms, expectations, and traditions of a life of hurry. We are starting to see that hurried living is a coverup when all along, throughout the generations, we have had God's gracious invitation to humankind. That is the invitation to breathe easier again. Jesus himself gives us the most beautiful invitation to slower living with rest for our weary souls. Come linger with me in these words:

We simply cannot keep holding our breath.

> Are you tired? Worn out? Burned out on religion? Come to me. Get away with me and you'll recover your life. I'll show you how to take a real rest. Walk with me and work with me—watch how I do it. Learn the unforced rhythms of grace. I won't lay anything heavy or ill-fitting on you. Keep company with me and you'll learn to live freely and lightly. (Matthew 11:28-30 MSG)

We Don't Have the Control After All

We are free to rest in the fact that we do not have as much control as we would like to think we do. We don't have to run away from our pain by staying busy. Fear can drive a lot of what we don't do. It's no secret that anxiety is rampant in our society: in our schools, our homes, our work, even in our leisure activities. And we also know that what goes unnamed goes undealt with. Carl Honoré, author of *In Praise of Slow,* says, "This is where our obsession with going fast and saving time leads. To road rage, air rage, shopping rage, relationship rage, office rage, vacation rage, gym rage. Thanks to speed, we live in the age of rage."

Pastor Kenny's Advent invitation that Sunday was a balm in a busy season as he offered these thoughts:

> Words are very important to God. Do not be afraid. Give God the recognition of your fear. This includes things you might need to finally change, a new kind of "casting all your fear" kind of trust that's rooted in these words from 1 Peter 5:7. It includes giving up control, and giving up what others will think of you.

It's perfectly fine to tell God you are tired and weary and need to exhale and rest. He wants to guide you.

I am more settled these days. I finally accepted that grief and joy do hold hands throughout life—when sea breeze and road rage collide. I understand that God kept me rooted in a nourished space. I was held in those rough waves. On the island. In the hospital. In my sunroom now. Like the curve out on I-85 in Atlanta, we will have unexpected pain ahead with new bends in the road we travel. However, you and I are being invited to walk with God. Every day. As if we are in the original garden again. A slow, lingering pace. Being present. Being attentive. Being in true community. Being at rest in a crazy world.

We get to gently, purposefully, and intentionally shift gears and fall into a rhythm that is more sustainable—that gives us room to breathe, keeping company with God, ourselves and others. This is a never-ending theme and a never-ending need in my life. I know it is in yours too, because you picked this book up. May you be empowered as you do the hard, sacred work of shifting and exhaling. Let's recover our time. We don't have to miss our one, precious life.

For Reflection and Discussion

Why is catching your breath important to you? What difference would it make?

What kind of experiences have disrupted your routine and your life, possibly bringing pain or heaviness along with them?

Are you afraid to slow down? If so, what do you think might be behind that fear?

2

Sometimes Slowing Down Is Chosen for You

The God who lifts us up through deep inner transformation is patient in his work, even when we aren't. Transformation takes time, but it is time spent building something of value.

ALAN FADLING

I REMEMBER SO VIVIDLY the stretch of time when my first husband, Brian, was fighting for his life after the truck accident. I was not getting much sleep. I often slept on a bench in the hospital corridor, right outside of the shock-trauma ICU. I'm one of those people who likes sleeping in the dark, but the lights never went off in the waiting area.

Stress was high during those months as I watched Brian suffer. I was scared to leave and go home because I was seeing so many families around me lose their loved ones. Being in a near-fatal car accident threatened to take Brian's life several times in the first few days, but his body kept going. And when someone lives when they probably should have died, it means that a brutal, long recovery ensues. So as those weeks turned into months, I became used to the back-and-forth life in a medical setting. Some days were spent boldly advocating for Brian's needs, and other times I was so tired that I barely knew what day it was.

One particular Friday night, after work, I noticed that there was a spot on the top of my foot that kept on itching. I knew it must be some kind of bug bite. A friend of mine took me to an urgent care facility, but the Benadryl they recommended did not help very much. By the next morning, I wasn't much better but managed to drive by myself, over an hour, to the teaching hospital Brian had been transferred to for a higher level of care.

My mother-in-law, a strong woman and fierce mama bear, who constantly blessed us both by advocating often on Brian's behalf, came to meet me in the hospital foyer. I asked her to look at my foot before I went upstairs to spend the weekend with Brian. I was relieved to see her, not just because she was a nurse but because I couldn't stop my alternating laughing and crying spells. Nothing would alleviate the itching on my foot—it was driving me bonkers. She was very bothered when she saw the big red streaks going up my leg. In my altered state and in my haste, I hadn't noticed those streaks or the gray square on top of my foot, like an embedded chip with a dot in the middle. We hurried over to the front desk and, before I knew it, there was a crew of smart young plastic surgeons all eyeing me.

The next thing I remember was waking up three days later, with my immediate family members all standing quietly around my bed in a private hospital room.

I suppose it's a good thing to be asleep and unaware while you are hooked up to IVs and the poison from a brown recluse spider is zapped out of you.

Maybe I should have felt blessed to have had the honor of being Sleeping Beauty for once in my life. But honestly, at the time I thought, "Seriously, Lord? Like I really need more drama this year? Inside of a huge hospital, over an hour from home!"

Looking back, I now see the clear, absolute timing and the sheer beauty of the hand of God. Allowing me to literally pause. It was the rest that my body craved but my mind would not hand over. What a divinely ordained respite—bringing our two families to the same building to be with us.

Through the years, I have pondered this whole "making something good out of something very bad" idea. Sometimes you can barely grasp hold of anything good. It's like your very breath itself is shallow. And other times, it takes years to realize that a bad situation may have been your only out. Providentially, a protection you weren't aware you needed. These are the times you exhale slowly

> *It was the rest that my body craved but my mind would not hand over.*

and shake your head. I mean, really? I certainly couldn't have planned my three-day siesta this way, that's for sure.

Slow Living Shift
Acceptance

Are you struggling with reconciling to something that just feels awful with no end in sight? Waiting with no light at the end of the tunnel can be one of the toughest things to face. But your story isn't finished being written yet. And that in itself is a beautiful thing to hold on to. A good word that I come back to often comes from Bob Goff. He says: "Embrace uncertainty. Some of the most beautiful chapters in our lives won't have a title until much later."

Through various seasons of having to slow down, to not be in control, and to move at a slower pace, the only thing that helped me see rest as a true gift was coming to a place of acceptance.

Often we cannot see what God is doing at the moment; we must trust. This posture of acceptance gave me the ability to have open hands. I started to slowly unpack the gift of rest and waiting that was often disguised as suffering.

The gift of nature is also something to not overlook when our bodies are forced to stop. Briny saltwater can even restore us. Whenever we were feeling under the weather on Bonaire, our island doctor, a very tall and robust Dutchman, would instruct us to go linger in the sea. The combination of rest, sun, and saltwater irrigation was always one of the best solutions, letting nature restore our bodies.

Slowing down has a way of shining the light on what's good in a situation. So often we cannot see what God is doing at the moment. In my case, I have had to shift from *telling* God what I need to *asking* God what I need.

When I tore my meniscus and had to have surgery, my third one, I couldn't believe it happened during the holidays, the busiest time of the year. I tried to recall earlier themes about slowing down and God saying, "Stay put for now." It wasn't easy. But it was easier to hear his still, small voice again, because my busyness and activity had been taken away. It was during this particular season that God inched me closer to a contemplative life led on purpose instead of by accident. Doors in my writing world started creaking open, providing opportunities that I had either walked past before or hadn't ever considered because my mind and body were so busy.

Bad Timing, Lord

Doesn't a forced pause always seem to happen at the most inopportune times? Not now, Lord, we tend to whisper loudly. I have noticed though, as I get older, that maybe I would do better to not resist these unchosen times of slowing down (and, often, solitude). Because really, in fighting so hard to move forward, I miss the chance to let my body and soul rest for a brief time. Savoring the pause is simply holding a posture of being resolved while not giving up. That holiday season, I learned that despite all the hype, the holidays did not actually have to be a frantic to be a nostalgic success, after all.

Whether we're in a beach chair or on bed rest, we can let God have the control back when we accept the season we are in. We can lean in and listen to what's next. Despite feeling like we are in a holding pattern, slowing down prepares us for the upcoming season of life. It gives us time to pause, to reflect, and to shift ideas. That doesn't happen when we're racing around. It also gives others a chance to do their thing, like love on us. Sometimes we need to be taken care of but can't see that we need help.

During my spider bite saga, I experienced rest and care in a way I never would have chosen for myself. Only after my recovery was I able to look back to see and accept the gift I had originally deemed an unfair and outrageous set of circumstances.

By the way, although most poisonous spider bites produce awful scars, I don't have one—and cannot even recall now which foot was bitten.

Not every hard experience leaves a scar. Sometimes we are changed from the inside, where a shift slowly starts to happen, like a large cruise ship turning around to find a better route in a majestic sea. I think it probably goes without saying that almost everyone we know has stood on the shores of a long season of slowing down, whether they wanted to or not. We have the choice to dismiss our story or accept it. Sometimes life's biggest waves knock us down and sometimes they clean us up.

> *Sometimes life's biggest waves knock us down and sometimes they clean us up.*

The entire world was certainly forced to slow down in March of 2020. Forced pauses can make us evaluate our priorities and help us not take things or people for granted. I wouldn't say the pandemic ushered in a shift so much as it brought life to a screeching halt. There was much suffering, darkness, and anxiety that came with it. And for all that was lost that we held dear, we still mourn.

But there was also a chance for a slow rebirth of sorts. Being present at home led to many dogs and cats being adopted from shelters. Families took longer walks, sometimes multiple times a day. Churches worked to go online, which resulted in the inclusion of people who normally couldn't make it to a service in person due to health issues or old age. Books were read, gardens were brought back to life, coffee was consumed, and neighbors reached out a helping hand.

And as life started shifting back to a new normal, to my amazement, women started telling me how they had truly loved cutting things out: social obligations that seemed never-ending, the extra work meetings, the unending gas needed in the car, the constant volunteering at church, running multiple errands per day, too many extra school activities, and more. They didn't know if they wanted to go back to the hustle of their former schedule and wondered if maybe they were never cut out for a fast-paced life to begin with. Just maybe, they had been doing what everyone else was doing even when it wasn't a good fit for their own family. Even when it was wearing them plumb out! The Great Pause certainly got people thinking about what they really wanted their family time, their health, their relationships, their churches, and their careers to look like.

When my husband, who works in corporate America, told me about the phenomenon of the "Great Resignation," I couldn't believe my ears. People were shifting away from the way things were always done. Many were quitting jobs to start their own businesses, follow their passions, and do the slow work of making their dreams come alive. Working from home and doing Zoom meetings had shown them that what was deemed important, an emergency, or "the way we've always done it" wasn't always true after all. Their eyes had been opened during the Great Pause, and they didn't want their life choices to be full of regrets. If Mary Oliver were here, she would most likely say: "Tell me what it is you plan to do with your one wild and precious life." It's a lot to ponder.

Many of us would willingly change things in our lives if given the time and the opportunity. Being forced to rest or reset got our attention and gave some of us that time and opportunity. I am seeing an underlying gratitude for a way out of a culturally dictated lifestyle which people felt stuck in.

Sometimes We Have to Let
Someone Else Carry Us

We don't usually plan for times when we need someone to step in and help us in a big way. But inevitably we will run into a season of life when we need to step away for rest. In God's provision, this is his gentle invitation to exhale. Sometimes we just have to let a friend carry us through the darkness, whether that's literally or figuratively. We have to accept help to slow down.

There are times when we find ourselves as the recipient of a grace so big it resembles arrows pointing to God himself. I have learned to not take neighbors for granted. I have also seen lavish graciousness poured out to me when I could never pay it back. The sheer gift of someone else's time, deep sacrifice, and kindness can be mind-blowing when you look back.

One of the most humbling experiences I can recall is being given the gift of time that was turned into a paycheck for me. It still overwhelms me. This happened during a long season where I could not work due to incredibly high stress. God sent me Laura at this time!

My friend offered to work my 9-to-5 reception job at our church's front desk while Brian was in the ICU. Days turned into weeks, which turned into months, and Laura sat at my desk, in my chair, and did my job. This in itself was an answer to prayer because I wanted to spend time with my critically injured husband.

But the gift kept getting bigger and deeper. Laura never saw a paycheck. The paychecks that should have been sent to her were routed to my bank account instead. It was like she was me. I can hardly think about this gift without tearing up, even many, many years later. It remains one of the biggest gifts I have received in this lifetime.

Laura not only met a huge need, but her selflessness played a part in my continued transformation as a Christ-follower. She helped shape my view of who God is with her generosity, impacting my life in profound ways.

We never know when God will call us to bring a loaf of fresh bread to a neighbor or when he will call us to work forty hours a week for another person who needs a respite or simply cannot function due to some kind of suffering. What we might view as the right thing to do or "doing it as unto the Lord" can mean the world to someone else. We get to be a part of someone feeling overwhelming gratitude when we do big and little things in this earthly kingdom. We have the honor of pointing another person to God.

Instead of being sad that I could never pay it forward in this capacity, I have accepted and chosen to be grateful for the label of recipient in this case—receiving an exhale I desperately needed so that I could rest and attend to other important things. I remain in complete wonder at how God sees us, offers us a way out, and uses other people to show us his magnificent love and care.

Looking Up

Do you find yourself in a dry spell—socially, spiritually, or physically? A season you didn't choose? I have been in long seasons where my health dictated my activities. Eighteen years of Hashimoto's disease brought in other autoimmune diseases, a good dose of fatigue, and the need to move at a slower pace to keep the stress level down. While I was understandably not always happy about this, I knew that I needed to find a way to be at peace when slowing down was chosen for me.

The changes we all experienced in the Great Pause came on quickly, tipping many of us off balance. I'll admit, the drastic shift in my routine and lifestyle, and what I had taken for granted all this time, threw me for a loop, causing me to question my writing vocation. I started to lose interest; fear of the unknown took over, and I thought I wanted to put my pen down.

You see, I had just recently hit a point where I proclaimed: "God, I don't know if anyone will want my book. You'll have to show me if I'm still supposed to write about this whole slowing down thing. What if people laugh? What if I can't craft my words as well as other authors? What if I fail? You'll have to show me what to do. Please give me a sign soon if you want me to keep going."

And lo and behold, on one of the many, many silent walks I took with my little dog in mid-2020, a special message appeared just for me. My answer from God arrived on the side of a freight train passing through our small town. This particular train was taking its sweet southern time. The shrill sound of the whistle and the clinking of metal on the tracks startled Bella; I scooped her up along with her leash and held her close. We stood still, feeling the vibration coming through the intersection and onto the sidewalk where we stood. And in slow motion . . . I looked up.

My eyes fixated on two words rolling by. They were spray-painted on the side of one of the old rusty train cars in the most beautiful, ocean-blue graffiti I had ever seen. (And there sure is a lot of bizarre and unsightly graffiti on those trains.) Can you even guess what it said?

It said: *slow life*.

I froze, gingerly watching it disappear over the bridge and into the woods nearby. With tears in my eyes, I squeezed Bella and asked her if she had seen the words too. Apparently she had not. I lifted my head to the sky and said "Thank you" out loud. God had heard me and had taken note of my request.

And so that day, I resolved to not close this chapter, but to start making steps to continue writing the best book I could on the soul benefits of slowing down, because I know how life-giving that shift is. The pages in this book aren't just a gentle reminder for myself, but an invitation and a lifeline for anyone who is desperately looking for God to give them words too. The transformed life includes these periods of stillness, of forced rest and of dreams paused. There is not a day that God does not see you, nor a month, or a year that is wasted in these forced pauses of life.

Frederick Buechner gracefully sums up how to hold the reality of those times when life slows down without our consent. He says: "Listen to your life. See it for the fathomless mystery it is. In the boredom and pain of it, no less than in the excitement and gladness: touch, taste, smell your way to the holy and hidden heart of it, because in the last analysis all moments are key moments, and life itself is grace."

For Reflection and Discussion

If you uncovered a gift during a time when slowing down was chosen for you, did you recognize this gift right away? Or did the acceptance come later?

What have you seen, heard, and observed when life has slowed you completely down?

Look at the Alan Fadling quote from the beginning of this chapter. Why do you think God is patient in our transformation?

3

A Sea Glass Transformation

And the God of all grace, who called you to his
eternal glory in Christ, after you have suffered
a little while, will himself restore you and
make you strong, firm and steadfast.

1 PETER 5:10 NIV

BEING OUTSIDE IN EIGHTY-DEGREE WEATHER all year gave me occasion to play in a large cove full of sea glass as a girl. The thousands of cobalt, ruby, emerald, and amber hues magnified under the crystal-clear water looked like gems to me. I can still hear the gentle back-and-forth swishing of the glass, sand, and pebbles that was almost hypnotic in that cove. Not to mention the bursts of sunlight shining through, creating a piece of sparkling art resembling the stained-glass church windows that I now love to gaze at as an adult.

When the sun's rays shift and hit sea glass, the glass piece sparkles, regardless of whether it's still a newly broken shard or a smooth, tumbled, and weathered piece of art. Just as sea glass can be tossed about and then transformed into something beautiful from the effects of rough sand, salty water, and time, our broken lives can also be transformed through hardship.

Sometimes life invites us to pause, reflect, and move forward in a new, transformed way.

Mary Beth Beuke, author and world-renowned sea glass expert, says:

> Like us, sea glass has been on a tumultuous journey. It's been broken first of all, then subsequently discarded into the sea or body of water. It has endured a wild journey and has been pummeled by storms, tossed by waves and tide and with the washing of briny, salt-water is always . . . wonderfully renewed.

The journey of sea glass becoming transformed is a story of both/and, much like our daily journey. The sea glass had an original purpose, most likely as a bottle. At some point, it was thrown away, either into a trash dump at the water's edge or from people sailing through the area. What may have started out as a fun three-hour tour, the glass bottle floating on the sparkling sea, most likely ended with this same bottle being thrown against the rocks and cliffs by incoming waves, shattering the smooth silhouette into sharp pieces. These shards tumble through the vast sea, get dragged around by currents along the sandy bottom, and bounce off rocks, shells, and coral, sometimes for years.

"Like us, sea glass has been on a tumultuous journey."

MARY BETH BEUKE

Seeing Beauty in the Broken

When we pick up a smooth piece of sea glass on a beach walk, turning it over in our hand, we are holding a piece whose jagged edges have been ground down by time and the elements.

Treasure hunters and collectors always seem to see the beauty in the broken. I attended a sea glass festival a few years ago to learn about this thriving, exciting industry; to say I was mesmerized would be an understatement.

The older I get, the more I am drawn to repurposed beauty, especially when natural light illuminates it. When I come across stained-glass windows, I find myself drawn into the story of the picture in those panes. I have pulled into a small church parking lot more than once to get a closer look, especially when the sun hitting the image just right has caught my eye. I'm intrigued by the story that is in front of me, made up of a rainbow of colors.

Slow Living Shift
Restoration and Reflection

One of the best things we can do is to hold space for ourselves and those around us as we move through both joys and sorrows. But to do this well, we must slow down. This invitation to hold space for the bumpy legs of the journey, for the broken parts of us, for the smooth and shiny days when the light hits just right, comes to all of us. We are given a daily opportunity to slow down and reflect. To pause and invite God to be present in the broken parts. To really see beauty and pain—making a place for it.

We can have an appreciation for the myriad of examples we heard about occurring in nature during 2020—a rebirth of sorts happening all around the world. Dolphins swimming in the clear European canals that used to hold dirty water. Animals spotted on greenways at parks where normally the crowds of people moving through quickly would have kept them in hiding. Air quality and pollution recorded at an all-time low. Living through global difficulties showed us a few things: without bursts of possibility and hope, there is nothing to look forward to. We need cracks of light to penetrate the darkness that often comes in waves.

We need cracks of light to penetrate the darkness that often comes in waves.

Through repetitious reflection we can find our hope and not grow discontent, which is easy to do.

Patience in the Darkness

Restoration takes time. We cannot hurry this transformation that slowly occurs. There will be some tough days as we shed the hustle culture we come from and find new ways of being in the world. Storms will be part of the journey.

Sometimes the sun breaks through the clouds like a flashlight on a dreary day, and the rays look like pathways. By the early light of dawn, mushrooms of all shapes and colors randomly pop up out of the soft, dark dirt in our backyard. They make me smile, as if they have something bold to exclaim.

In Barbara Brown Taylor's book *Learning to Walk in the Dark,* she talks about embracing the dark as a part of life. What if we grew up not being afraid to turn the lights off, instead of always associating the darkness with evil, fear, or confusion? What if in our solitude and darkness, we came to finally believe that we are really not alone?

While we cannot feel God's presence warming us like the sun, we can see his light illuminating the darkness and bringing us home, like a moonbeam lighting the path in a dark wood. What if the darkness holds the opportunity to hold our heavenly Father's hand in a way we might not in the light?

The story goes that not once, but on two separate occasions as a little girl, I reached up and grabbed a stranger's hand in the dark, thinking it was my father's hand. When the lights came on, I looked up in total surprise, realizing my dad was actually a few feet away from me. And that tells me that I instinctively knew that if my dad was near, I was safe in the dark; he would hold my small hand. We sometimes get so busy that we forget that God is near. It was A. W. Tozer who said, "We need never shout across the spaces to an absent God. He is nearer than our own soul, closer than our most secret thoughts."

We have been through times when we yearned for light to break through the dark seasons of our collective days. I wonder what my interactions with others would be like if I could remember that they might be holding two opposite truths in their pocket. It might not be written all over their face. I might not guess correctly if I assume the smile they give me is the only indication of the good life I think they are living.

You may recall a time when you felt two opposite emotions within a very short timeframe. I can vividly remember sitting at a family Easter luncheon, feeling grateful for the chance to gather over a beautiful meal, only to choke back hot tears because holidays stirred up a not-often-talked-about sadness I felt from missing people who were no longer sitting at the table.

When everyone is wearing their Sunday best, spring flowers are in bloom, and the ham and deviled eggs are being passed around, it is jolting to our minds and our hearts to be flooded with an old memory or a current reality that is harsher than we would like.

Healing fresh or old wounds and celebrating big or little things are best experienced when we slow down to take it all in and hold space for both. After all, this is our present reality.

The stories we hold—of sorrow and joy, longing and contentment, anticipation and regret, anxiety and serenity—can feel so heavy at times that we think we disgrace one if we honor the other. But we can indeed honor both narratives by letting the emotions come when they come. We dishonor our experiences when we try to gloss over them and stick a thankfulness Band-Aid on the wound.

Remaking involves holding space for the past, present, and future. While we don't want to dwell on the past, the truth is, some pieces of it will always be with us. Reflecting speaks into our transformation, allowing us to slow down, sifting and choosing what we take with us into the future. I have learned much from Alan and Gem Fadling, friends and peers who have long been writing and coaching about the benefits of living an unhurried life. One of my favorite concepts to sit with comes from their cowritten book *What Does Your Soul Love?* They write, "We move at the pace of grace and we grow at the pace of transformation."

Sea glass takes several decades to get its new shape and texture. It can even take up to a whole century to change from shiny, slick glass to a weathered, mostly frosted appearance. Just like the transformation of a piece of sea glass, slower living is this invitation to reframe our heartache as we take our tossed-about lives and repurpose our pace into a more manageable and delightful one. We get to experience a more natural ebb and flow as we accept this wild invitation to slow down, pause, and hold space for ourselves. This in turn, gives us the opportunity to hold space for another person in their darkness, in their remaking.

The balancing of different emotions—and holding space for others around you who are doing the same, day in and day out—is a true gift and cannot be learned or lived out in a hurried way. Transformation is an invitation to slow down. May we let those cracks of light shine through. And even in the darkness, may someone feel our warmth as they feel hope slowly but surely reaching back for them.

> *Transformation is an invitation to slow down.*

For Reflection and Discussion

Do you collect something from nature, like sea glass? If so, what is the before-and-after journey each piece takes?

Can you remember a time when you walked alongside someone and held space for them through their sorrow or unanswered questions? What do you recall?

Tell about a time when the light hit an object or scene just right and illuminated something unexpected or new for you.

4

You Are Exactly Who
You Are Supposed to Be

Honoring the capacity and pacing of those around us is a way to affirm their inherent dignity. Honoring our personal capacity and pacing is a way to affirm our own.

AUNDI KOLBER

SOME OF US LOVE TO GO FAST. We are wired to get things done. If you are like this, you may be reading this book because you want to learn to slow down or you want to understand a loved one who does not move as fast as you do. You are welcome.

Some of us do not have it in us to hustle. Some of us need more quiet or require extra time. We are built that way. And yet, not everyone likes the way we need to move in the world. So sometimes we start equating our worth and likability with productivity—how fast we move and how much we can get done.

I had never associated my dignity with the act of honoring my capacity or my pace until I pored over the above quote by author and trauma therapist Aundi Kolber. Aundi's work has impacted my own life, and her gentleness speaks volumes. I felt such a relief to not feel shame or unworthiness because of my inability to move as fast as someone else. My definition of productivity may look different from someone else's, for a variety of reasons unique to me. What we believe about our own sense of belonging will be shaped by how we view ourselves, so I am learning to be gentle.

Weariness, health struggles, sadness, and even the weather can cause us to lack energy for what we feel should be easy. Sometimes life might feel easy enough. But there will be many more seasons when we let expectations dictate the time we give to others. The heavy load we think we should carry effortlessly and quickly can bring on powerful shame, even if it's not rational.

A while back, I looked at my schedule and decided to step out of my comfort zone by joining a weekly strength training class at our local recreational center. Since I hadn't done strength training in a long time, I felt awkwardness rising. I hoped I could hide my weaknesses in a room full of strangers in yoga pants. When I came to the first class, a woman walking in behind me asked if I was going to the class. "I hope it won't be too hard for me!" she added. It seemed appropriate in that moment to show compassion for her bandwidth and mine. Smiling, I told her to do what she has the energy and capacity for. No one was competing—everyone would be at a different level.

Knowing and honoring my personal limits prompted me to take breaks and not feel guilty. It really helped that my friend and accountability partner Lindsay would be there; I didn't want to let her down. But even in our shared commitment, we were able to give each other grace, encouraging each other to show up to be our best selves when we had the capacity for it. If one of us was too tired for class, we showed each other kindness rather than judgment.

One time, a song came on during class—one that I had listened to on long, lonely road trips during a season of mourning. It triggered an enormous sadness in me that I couldn't shake, so I left early to sit outside and get some fresh air until Lindsay came to check on me. My empathy and high sensitivity were activated by the music and memories. If you've had this happen to you when you've least expected it, there is nothing wrong with you. Some people just react strongly to art, music, and nature.

We can look at a large purple dumbbell and see that it's heavy, but our own private loads are often invisible. It's hard to shake the feeling that you should be able to handle everything that comes your way. Embracing our level of capacity takes a weight from our collective shoulders. It's a good way to practice compassion for the unique ways we come to the table of life.

Slow Living Shift
Embracing Your Uniqueness

Many women and men feel shame and doubt, wondering if they are weaker than, or built differently from, peers who seem to move fast and have it all together, bounding with endless energy. They may have traits like high sensitivity, empathy, or introversion—strong characteristics that allow us to live more authentically and attentively in the world but also come with their own challenges. It may also be that an illness holds you back—whether visible or invisible. If you are sensing freedom to pause or to exhale for the first time in a very long time, it may be that you have these traits or health limitations, and no one has acknowledged that you must move a bit slower. Your unique traits are actually a gift. Your life circumstances are your reality. No matter what you may have heard from others, I believe you are not "too much."

There is nothing wrong with your deep longing to move at your desired pace and not go back to the hustle you may have been in. My own body simply couldn't keep up with societal norms. You may have compensated for so many things that you don't even realize your need to shift to this slower pace is not something to apologize for, but actually to embrace!

Your unique traits are actually a gift.

Your path is not supposed to look like her path. Your ideas are not supposed to mirror her ideas. Your wiring is not supposed to feel like her wiring. Slow down. Lean in. Look up. And journey on.

Ways We Are Unique

Highly sensitive people. Six years ago, I learned that I was likely a "highly sensitive person." Andre Sólo and Jenn Granneman, creators of Sensitive Refuge, define a highly sensitive person (HSP) as "someone who has high sensitivity to the sights, sounds, emotional cues, and other stimuli around them." After researching this phenomenon more by reading books and articles, and finding a nearby HSP therapist, I finally felt permission to accept myself for the first time in my life. What a pure gift that was and such a relief to name it! I had been this way since I was three years old and wasn't sure why certain things bothered me that did not seem to faze others. Now, many more therapists are becoming aware of high sensitivity.

I have found that being an HSP means that things irritate or distract me that might not bother other people. Bright lights, loud or startling noises, strong smells, crowded gatherings, and extreme heat or cold are just some of the things that not only make me move more slowly but cause me to pause and take inventory of my surroundings. This allows life to be more enjoyable and tolerable.

Twenty percent of us function at our best when we embrace slower living. Elaine Aron, author of *The Highly Sensitive Person*, says that one in five people are highly sensitive. For the highly sensitive person, feeling overstimulated is a way of life.

High sensitivity runs in the family, believe it or not! When I explained more about my sensitivities to my parents, they not only understood because they had observed it all these years, but my dad nodded and said, "Ah! I think I understand some things about my own mother more now." Naming things gives freedom and understanding. Who knew that my grandmother, who I never got to spend much time with, was so much like me? That knowledge alone increased my feeling of belonging—a deep longing I had had over the span of my life to be seen and acknowledged in a society where I had felt too sensitive or high-maintenance for most of my life.

For the most part, people like to be accommodating. I now speak up if I'm riding in the car as a passenger and the music is too loud. It's not a matter of complaining to mention it; it's a reasonable request. My brain cannot always tune out the lyrics, so it's like listening to two conversations at the same time. It's even more difficult when the speaker is facing forward in the car, instead of facing me like in a regular conversation. Just as a back seat passenger asking for their window to be rolled up is not a complaint but a reasonable request, we who are highly sensitive can graciously ask for what we need. This act of asking for what I need helps me to be more present to hear the driver. Slowing down to be attentive to each other is important and usually creates a win for everyone!

High empathy. Empathetic people don't always move as fast in the world because they are busy taking in so many stimuli: reading the room when they walk into a location, sensing what others are feeling, and often using up their own energy reserves to emotionally care for others. Empathy is a great trait to have and is considered a strength in many professional circles. But while high empathy is not a bad thing, it is nonetheless draining.

I need to take great care to replenish my energy levels so I can be my best self for everything else going on in my day. I once ran around the neighborhood in the wrong shoes, helping a boy look for his lost dog. I've listened and teared up as a new friend poured out her life story. Those activities drained me—even though I was happy to help. There seems to be a cost to having high empathy, yet most of us wouldn't trade it for the world. We intuitively appreciate this way of seeing those we love, not to mention the unlocking of our creative side that we might not have otherwise.

Empathy is especially needed in times of distress and grief. Author Clint Watkins gives us something to contemplate. He says, "Whether out of love or self-preservation, we can inadvertently pressure others to polish their pain. But gospel hope compels us to be patient with others' heartache. Resurrection, by nature, requires waiting."

For almost forty years, I thought that my high empathy was a weakness. I wasted a great deal of time and emotion fighting against this beautiful trait before understanding it was one of my greatest strengths—something God had put in me.

Introversion. Those of us who are introverts often tend to move slower as well. We take our time in social settings and feel drained by too much emotional and physical giving and receiving. Introverts are unlikely to find a quiet evening at home lonely; rather, alone time allows for refreshment, recharging, and engaging in activities. Sometimes introverts need to process things longer. If you're an introvert, know that it's okay to take the time you need to get your bearings, understand something, get clarity, or make a decision.

Our personality as well as our frame of mind shapes how we view being alone; whether we welcome it as a gift or view it as a curse. As Hoda Kotb writes, "You come home, make some tea, sit down in your armchair, and all around there's silence. Everyone decides for themselves whether that's loneliness or freedom."

What comes to mind for you when you picture yourself sitting down in that armchair? Are you feeling lonely and isolated or grateful for a quiet pocket of time? Afraid or content? Tired or bored? Are you being refreshed in mind, body, and spirit? Do you have the urge to dim the lights and settle in?

Susan Cain, who started the Quiet Movement, has a TED Talk with over thirty-three million views. Her topic? *The Power of Introverts.* In her talk, Susan says that "a third to a half of the population are introverts—a third to a half. So that's one out of every two or three people you know."

Our culture often scoffs at personalities who require more time, space, and solitude to function. There is an extremely large number of introverts who wonder if anyone sees them. I am raising my own hand here. Whether this is you or someone you love, knowing that there is nothing wrong with the way you move through the world is a key to empowerment. It unlocks the freedom to finally advocate for yourself to find a sustainable pace in a busy world.

Chronic illness and invisible illness. Many people suffer from chronic illnesses like cancer, diabetes, stroke, heart disease, or arthritis. These illnesses are debilitating and can wear our bodies down, giving us no choice but to slow way down for long seasons. The good news is that most people, if they know somebody is experiencing illness, will understand the inability to produce or function at a high capacity.

But chronic illness isn't the only thing slowing many of us down. The number of people with invisible illnesses—illnesses where the person doesn't outwardly exhibit signs of being sick—is quite common. Many times, such individuals are left floundering in social circles where hustle and productivity often overshadow the simple act of just sitting with someone in their new uninvited health journey. Creating the space and acceptance for a healthier pace and not feeling like you are "too much" for needing this is pivotal to thriving in society. After all, we all move to a certain rhythm. It can be frustrating when someone comments that you "look fine"— insinuating that there is nothing wrong with you when your body is screaming at you to pay attention to the subtleties of your pain.

This might resonate with many of you. It's hard to feel like talking to others about your limitations. Whether they are visible or invisible to so many people around you, it's tiring to try to explain yourself, receive unsolicited advice, or answer personal questions. While each of us can show kindness to one another at different levels, embracing empathy helps us to more fully see the pain a friend has had in his or her own life, and the need to hold space for their questions and lonely days.

I see you through a more compassionate lens than I would have many years ago. I've had years of adrenal fatigue. And within a year of being widowed, almost twenty-five years ago, I developed Hashimoto's, an inherited autoimmune disease. Several knee surgeries, daily joint pain, reduced lung capacity, and more blend together in seen and unseen ways. But all of it causes me to listen to my body and set a gentler pace for myself as the day plays out. For me, losing time and productivity is a reality, but too much striving negatively affects my quality of life.

* * *

Coming to peace with the wiring of those around us and ourselves lends itself to much contentment. It's not as lonely to walk your own path when you can hold your head up high because you are living authentically to how you were made. As you embrace who you are, you will pave the way for others who are watching you to be fully themselves, which is a gift in itself.

The word *dignity* means to treat someone as being of worth, being respectful and kind, and listening to what they say or how they act. Just as not every disappointment necessarily holds a lesson to be learned, not every opportunity necessarily holds a demand to participate, be stronger, go faster, or press harder. Look at your uniqueness and see if your gifts and ability to enhance the world aren't looking right back at you, smiling!

Not every disappointment necessarily holds a lesson to be learned.

As our bodies seem to remember our trauma, many of us need to continually recharge our energy levels. If our hearts are weighed down with the suffering we see in the world, we can choose to be gentle with ourselves. It's more than fine that we cannot tolerate what someone else can. Reducing noise level, conflict, social media, or news stories can be a healthy way to meet ourselves with care.

It seems fitting to reflect on a valuable line of thought in Aundi Kolber's book *Try Softer*. She says: "We are invited to cease white-knuckling, because though it once kept us physically or emotionally safe, a new and gentler way is open to us."

For Reflection and Discussion

How has your need to pace yourself affected how you move in the world when you feel pressured to move quickly?

How do you view these sometimes-disregarded strengths—high sensitivity, high empathy, being an introvert, feeling things deeply, or needing to move slower—in light of your own circumstances?

What can you start doing to honor your pace? Or the pace of a friend?

5

Understanding Capacity

*We need a rest—a cessation of waves long enough
for us to catch our breath. Sometimes I think we're
alone in this sea, but when I turn to the women
around me, the scent of saltwater clings to their
bodies. Their hair is damp with their own pain.
Their souls bear the carving out of wave after wave.*

KIMBERLY COYLE

CULTURE DEFINES THE WAYS WE VIEW each other and
what our expectations and demands are of one another. Often,
here in the United States, we have an idea that there is no option
but to push hard and fast, to accommodate others in this fast-
paced world while ignoring our own aches and slow unraveling.
We believe others want us to move quickly and say yes to unrealistic requests. It is often assumed that most of us want bigger
and better. Examining who and what is telling us to hurry is an
important step in taking back agency in our lives. Understanding
our capacity is a good starting point.

Not every culture hustles. We did not have a traffic light on
the island. I vividly remember being behind a car whose driver
stopped to talk to another driver. Both men leaned in toward

open windows, smiling, carrying on. And guess what? My dad and I had to just wait to drive on until their conversation was done. While that might be unthinkable in bustling cities, it was a way of life on Bonaire. We called this pace *poco-poco*. It is a connection; the in-between of here to there. A slowness that is built into this salty air culture.

Who Is Keeping You from Slowing Down?

We often believe the lie that speed is the only way to move through life or to get ahead. But really, who is keeping you from slowing down? It is a unique dance between others' expectations and what we perceive and believe in our own minds. We are afraid that we may be "left behind" or forgotten, like a small child stopping to see every animal at the zoo. But in reality, slowing down is a radical act of courage as we work to unlearn previous beliefs. Let's put forth due diligence to deconstruct some of the myths and lies about hustle and productivity, so that we get to construct and follow our own life-giving rules and rhythms.

But really, who is keeping you from slowing down?

We who are entrusted with our homes, our children, our small businesses, our careers, our communities, our aging parents, our finances, our health, and so much more these days, cannot afford "not to" curb the voracious pace in our society. When your body is screaming at you to rest, whether via a massive headache, heart palpitations, anxiety, overwhelm, or fatigue, this is an alarm to pay attention and shift priorities. The burnout in trying to do more than we have capacity for is part of the price we are paying for believing the lie that we need to do it all to be strong, competent humans.

What Are You Afraid Will Happen If You Do Slow Down?

There are many myths about slowing down. We aren't allowed to rest because that is laziness. No one will come forward to take the job you just walked away from, so you are needed. Everything must be done today. You're letting everybody down. Boundaries are selfish. This chapter could no doubt be titled "Running On Empty From the Lies We've Believed."

Here are some truths about slowing down: slow down and your passions that have been tucked in for too long will start to emerge. Your body will pick up on the cues that it's safe to start recovering and replenishing. You'll start seeing people in front of you in a totally different way. Your world and the hidden beauty all around you will come alive! You will recover your one precious life and create space for the things that really matter to you and your family. When the pain of being weary and worn out is greater than the fear of missing out or letting someone down, you know you have started the biggest shift of all toward slower living.

When the pain of being weary and worn out is greater than the fear of missing out or letting someone down, you know you have started the biggest shift of all toward slower living.

We can read a lot about this idea of productivity. It's looked different in many places around the world during various centuries. This idea of faster and more started to really come about in the United States during the Second Industrial Revolution. Eric Niiler, a science and climate reporter points out, "The rapid advancement of mass production and transportation made life a lot faster. From the late 19th to early 20th centuries, cities grew, factories sprawled, and people's lives became regulated by the clock rather than the sun." Sadly, the rage against moving slowly has long infiltrated churches, schools, businesses, homes, and hearts, and affects all of us. But there is an awakening happening.

Something inside of you knows you were made for so much more, but the definition of more has become skewed because of the low-hanging clouds of smoke billowing from the hub of the often invisible machine. Unhelpful and obsolete ideas that have become normalized over time, regardless of their benefits, will start deteriorating, often in plain view all around us. We just don't always see it until the damage has been done.

It's past time for releasing regrets, expectations, certain relationships, and shame because of the idea that more is better and faster. I think sometimes we don't know what we're missing. We are in our own timeline, not aware that outside of the factory, the rest of the world doesn't necessarily run like us. I find it interesting that so much of this faulty theology may have been placed on us by a well-oiled machine that never understood our pace and still doesn't.

Slow Living Shift
Understanding Capacity

While it's honorable to have open hands and want to help others, getting a proper perspective on how your body and mind are doing is important. That's why this easy tool below is so eye-opening. If you are trying to determine whether you have the bandwidth, the energy, and the capacity to say yes to something new or last minute, visualizing a container that holds your capacity is super helpful and gives you a truer picture. It's amazing how a scallop, a coconut, a pitcher, and a bucket can help us make clearer decisions in life!

In the following section, I show you how I walk clients through the first part of a slow living session. We start by filling in the Reflection Guide so we can name things properly and see where they might really fit. Putting it down on paper offers a clearer picture of what is making one weary and what to do to unload the heavy stress.

Your Slow Living Shift: A Quarterly Reflection Guide

Sometimes it takes a little bit of time to decide what rhythms in your life need to stay or go. A simple tool has personally guided my rhythms since 2015. I created the one-page reflection tool at the end of this chapter when I was helping a friend decide if she should step down from a volunteer position that was taking a lot of time away from her family. What seemed like a beautiful opportunity to serve others two years prior was now draining energy from important relationships and other obligations. It was time to shed light on what needed shifting to create space for what fit in her new pace and smaller bandwidth. We all have what I call our seasons of sustainability. Thoughtfully and intentionally list your activities for this current season you are in, in their appropriate boxes, using the personal Reflection Guide at the end of this chapter.

There are four categories set in boxes in the Reflection Guide:

Obligations: what I must do; my reasonable yeses

Life-Giving Rhythms: natural, sustainable activities I really enjoy

Life Drainers: these wear me out; I don't even want to be doing this

Boundaries: I can say no; perhaps these are activities with built-in end dates

There is no wrong way to fill this out or a wrong season to start this. You can go through the quadrant every three months, or you could fill it out every month, reflecting on the last thirty days. Be sure you keep up with your life changes.

It may be helpful to have a safe, trusted friend look at the Reflection Guide with you. You may have a hobby or passion that is welling up inside of you but think you aren't supposed to make time for it. Your friend may suggest that you put it in the *Life-Giving Rhythms* box and see what happens. Ultimately, you will know best how your time commitments and your life

> *We all have our seasons of sustainability.*

rhythms could look. Let's take a look at Amanda filling out her guide, as her friend Beth sits at the table with her.

Reflection Guide Example

Amanda pulls out her Reflection Guide and thinks through how she is feeling, noting where the stress seems to reside in her body. She is a forty-year-old schoolteacher who pours herself out daily to her first-grade students. While she loves her job, Amanda is beginning to resent the extra volunteer jobs her administrator has added to her calendar. Amanda is starting to tire out more easily these days and realizes she needs some down time in the late afternoons. She is hopeful that this guide will help her to name this feeling of being pulled in too many directions. Amanda is at the point where she is ready to start her shift to slower living. So she lists after-school jobs in the *Life Drainers* box of her Reflection Guide.

Even as Amanda is feeling quite stretched right now, she has decided to focus on caring for her elderly mother at sporadic times during her week and weekend. She lists this in the *Obligations* box of her Reflection Guide. She knows this season will not be permanent and is honored to be in her mother's life. Amanda particularly loves hearing old family stories that are new to her. As her mother talks, Amanda jots down these treasured tales. She lists this experience in the *Life-Giving Rhythms* box on her guide, noting her own interest in journaling and family history.

Amanda feels pressure from someone in the ladies' group at her church to be part of a new weekly Bible study on the other side of town. Her friend Beth knows that it's hard for Amanda to say no to people, but she is aware of Amanda's scallop-shell capacity right now. Amanda lists the Bible study invitation in the *Life Drainers* box to remind her to curb her people-pleasing tendency when it pops up.

While leaving the house on a weeknight may have been appealing in another season, Amanda really wants to take up painting two evenings a week instead. She lists "painting" in the *Life-Giving Rhythms* box. When she paints in the quiet of her house, it feels life-giving to her. It's like a form of therapy: her hands can move and her mind can think through some big decisions she'll have to make with her mother soon. Amanda has also stumbled on a podcast where the host is reading through the Bible in a year, and she is excited about the idea of hearing someone reading Scripture to her in this season of higher stress. She lists these podcast episodes in the *Life-Giving Rhythms* box right along with her new art hobby.

Beth reminds Amanda that she can easily shift the painting to another night if she has to take care of her mother unexpectedly. But being out several nights a week could be more draining than helpful right now. Amanda looks at the *Life Drainers* box and decides to move the women's Bible study over to the *Boundaries* box to remind herself that she can confidently decline attending the Bible study during this season of life.

Amanda's shoulders relax. She already feels more in control of her schedule with this new tool. The ability to see what is taking up her time and what she can say no to in this season is freeing, and she is more full of hope than she has been in a long time.

When we are able to see things visually, we're at an advantage by having a bird's-eye view of our own life. Remember to fill this Reflection Guide out quarterly as so much can change from season to season in our personal and work lives. This is curated just for you, so it needs to fit your actual life, not what you think others expect from you. Make sure it is reasonable in all aspects.

For Reflection and Discussion

Fill in your Reflection Guide on the next page.

My Reflection Guide

OBLIGATIONS

What I must do

LIFE-GIVING RHYTHMS

Things I enjoy

LIFE DRAINERS

I'm worn out

BOUNDARIES

I can say no

6

Awakening to Beauty

This is the season she will make beautiful things.
Not perfect things but honest things
that speak to who she is and who she is called to be.

MORGAN HARPER NICHOLS

I HAVE ALWAYS BEEN A WRITER. And as a writer, I never want to abandon my craft for too long, yet last year I found myself in a holding pattern where the words seemed stuck and distant. Around the same time, I had this urge to buy watercolor paints, brushes, and special paper to find out if I could create with colors and texture instead of words. I was afraid that I wouldn't be any good at it and wanted to test the waters to see. I used to think that I wasn't as creative as other people until I discovered that I, too, was creative when given the proper time and space for ideas to surface and blossom.

My teenage daughter was sweet to sit with me for hours as I worked on what first looked to me like a kindergarten project while she did advanced and detailed art. I soon found out that this activity was relaxing and that the paint was forgiving. I loved how less water would give life to the vibrant colors and that a delightful image could emerge from a blank piece of paper. As I sat and painted, I wondered if I had wasted precious time putting off my writing and taking up a frivolous activity. But I soon found, to my utter surprise, that I wasn't terrible at it. I hadn't given myself much credit, but the work and fun produced an inner healing and quiet confidence in me.

After getting the need to paint out of my system for several weeks, my words began to flow once again onto the paper. This often emerged as a thought scrawled with a pen on a sticky note or typed on my computer at my desk in my sunroom. Often the words came out like a torrential downfall, where I'd leave myself a voice memo rambling a series of ideas that had flashed by and begged to be saved.

Slow Living Shift

Awakening to Beauty

We are multilayered, just like an oil painting. When God created the world, he said that it was good. When he created us, he announced that we were very good. There is a beloved beauty inside of us and all around us if we will shift our focus and pause long enough to behold it. The awakening will not unfold as fast as we would like, as there is a lot of undoing and unlearning to be done alongside this shifting.

We aren't a one-size-fits-all kind of people. Our personalities have texture and depth. There is a story unfolding in each one of us. My friend Cheryl says that as an adult, she has to loosen the chains of critics, boundaries, and limits to reset her creativity. The more she lets go of needing her art to be "good," the more the art becomes what it was meant to be. As she lets her creativity breathe, it regains its pulse and movement.

What would happen if, like Cheryl with her art, you started paying attention to the quiet rumblings that moved into a gentle nudge, awakening your creativity? What if you truly believed that your unique self was made in the image of the Creator who delights in you and sings over you? Would room to breathe infuse a fresh wind in your sails? Would it start to unlock a spark or a fire that has laid dormant for years? Would you respond to the invitation that is beckoning you to step out and try your hand at something you had laid down long ago? Or maybe something you never even believed you could do? What would that be? If you haven't considered this, it might take a few days for your heart to feel free enough to dare to create. Be curious. Be still. Have open hands to the wonder and see what blooms.

We Are God's Masterpiece

One of the most profound writing assignments I have ever worked on was in a virtual class back in 2021. My creative writing coach, Maile Silva, asked each of us in her class to imagine God speaking a blessing over us—his creation—when he formed us. I wondered what God said as he formed me. Did I resemble a piece of pottery? A sonnet? An oil painting? What about a sand-castle? A rose garden? A shooting star? Or possibly a stained-glass window? What I wrote surprised me: the words held beauty as well as the weight of things I never would have chosen for myself, both marvelous and horrific. Is it possible that when God created us, his eyes looked right at us, and his smiling face was indeed shining upon us? Maybe as a way of saying, "I see you, my child, and you are wonderfully made."

I wondered what God said as he formed me.

I share this finished poem below—a piece of my own creative awakening, as a vulnerable stance. I hope it is a guide for you and encourages you to contemplate, then write what you think God was thinking when he created you—his masterpiece.

> May this child's turquoise eyes as deep as the sea she will
> swim in
> See untold beauty in my creation of both nature and people
> May this child's white, blonde hair bleached from the
> noonday sun
> Bring unique delight to those around her
> May this child's alabaster skin handed down from her
> Dutch ancestors
> One day feel the winds of change brush over her
> and stand in solidarity with humankind
> May this child's heart formed by me to hold feelings
> of empathy
> Never harden as stone in a world marred by grief and
> suffering
> May this child's smile, while shy and inviting
> Be the catalyst for peacemaking and not peacekeeping
> May this child's bent towards lingering and listening in a
> loud world
> Help others feel seen and heard as deeper community
> is forged

May this child's gentleness and high sensitivity to chaos
Lead others back to me for rest and comfort
May this child's need for connectedness and love
Always be anchored in my love for her, my lovely creation.

What do you think God was thinking when he made you? I invite you to jot down a few things that come to mind in a journal, just as I did in my class. Or write your own poem.

Art in any form requires a process. First the blank piece of paper. Then the colors adorning the canvas one by one. Then an emerging masterpiece. A Polaroid film has to be in the dark before it shows what was captured in the light. A ceramic piece of pottery goes through much twisting, shaping, and heat to boldly hold contents. For art to come to life, to awaken, there is a before and after. This reminds me of the tension we hold when we think about the "already but not yet" in our Christian faith.

We are in the process of becoming. We are constantly shifting in some way or another. Some days we feel unique and altogether lovely, like a one-of-a-kind opus, and other days we feel less than, not enough, or invisible. Some days we need friends to tell us there's nothing wrong with us because we have forgotten our worth and our belovedness. Ephesians 2:10 (NLT) tells us, "For we are God's masterpiece. He has created us anew in Christ Jesus, so we can do the good things he planned for us long ago." Philippians 1:6 says that until Christ returns, we are literally a work in progress. There is a spaciousness in the both/and. So, we keep learning. We keep growing.

As many of us have started to slow down, we have become more aware of beauty and long to replicate that beauty. Have you needed a fresh start, a remolding, a blooming—but knew that moving fast would only cripple the attempt to come alive once again? When we move too fast through life, we forget what delights us and sets our souls on fire.

Books, podcasts, documentaries, and art galleries can also rouse the beauty inside of us. Almost fourteen years ago, God introduced me to the words of Ann Voskamp, primarily in her book *One Thousand Gifts*. I was thirsty for beauty, for meaning, and for life-giving words. This book was another tool God used to slow me back down and turn my gaze back to him. I suppose, in a way, it was a piece of what shifted me back toward the beauty I had once been immersed in on the island. Turning the pages, I accompanied Ann to the fields where the moonlight shone on her farm, illuminating the crops. Her lyrical words were my awakening. Once you see beauty, you can't seem to unsee it and you want to continue tracking it down.

We Can Learn from the Sea

When I was in elementary school, I was given the opportunity to have my picture taken underwater at the pier where our swim lessons were being held. The photographer's name was Dee Scarr, and I was fascinated by her camera gear and how it worked under the saltwater. As I posed and did a few turns and flips, she froze the moment in time for me, showing off the hues of blue sea and the barnacles that were attached to the pier wall behind me.

Although I do not know where that photograph is today, I recently looked Dee up on the internet. I was thrilled to see that not only is she the author of a book called *Touch the Sea*, but to learn she is referred to as the woman who "transformed dive tourism into a gentle discipline." Instead of disrupting reefs with photo ops and souvenir collection, Dee's approach focused on leaving the sea "as natural and pristine as possible." How remarkable that her work reframed diving as "discipline"—training and knowledge, a word descending from the root "to learn."

There is a "learning to be" that comes with letting the vastness and flow of deep water encompass you as you set out to find beauty. There is no fast way to scuba dive; the entire purpose is to linger, letting your body relax as you slowly breathe in and out of your regulator and take in the wonder all around you. Water is not just refreshing, it's restorative; and, in the case of diving, we are gently immersed and held under the sea. Bonaire has been known as a diver's paradise for years now because it offers some of the best scuba and snorkeling waters in the world.

Famous underwater filmmaker Jacques Cousteau called the ocean the "silent world." In this silence, there is a transformation that happens every time the sun goes down and dusk comes. While I have not visited the reef at night, I've been told that under the water, ordinary things you can see in daylight transform into a whole new world in the darkness. Even kicking your fins while swimming at night produces sea sparkle, from the plankton known as *Noctiluca scintillans*.

Biologist Chetana Purushotham says:

When the sun sets for the day, the ocean undergoes a dramatic transformation in appearance and animal activity. The mere disappearance of light creates a whole new set of unique challenges for marine life. Not being able to see, for instance, renders attributes like colourfulness (the hallmark of reef life) almost entirely useless at night. In coping with darkness, the evolution of the night shift has brought about some of the most incredible adaptations in animal senses, behaviors, and communities. Nocturnal life often rivals what you would imagine lived in outer space.

While night diving, you can be entranced and transported to another place where wonder abounds amid the silence. The sheer beauty of the watery underworld awakening at night brings avid scuba divers to Bonaire over and over again.

When Was Your Creative Awakening?

Often an experience when we are younger sets the stage for creativity to flourish as an adult. Whether that is something mysterious in nature, an encounter with an animal, or even in my case, a fifth-grade teacher who threw open the doors to awe and wonder, color and words. This richness in the creative world brings a level of wonder to everyday life, allowing us to be our authentic selves, use our unique giftings and appreciation for the world to shape our passions, our outlook, and our daily rhythms. When was your creative awakening? Do you remember what age you were?

My own creative awakening came in elementary school. Mrs. Perenboom, a Dutch woman married to our island dentist, was a true creative. "Perenboom" means "pear tree," and I cannot help but think that her life resembled the sturdy tree; she doled out sweet gifts from her own branches to us that year. She had survived breast cancer and was full of life. And she seemed to want to pass that vibrancy on to our class.

I remember the sense of awe the day we walked into class: our three-part chalkboard filling the front of the classroom had been transformed into a scene in an underwater adventure. Imagine a still version of an IMAX movie, but in the late 1970s. Mrs. Perenboom's reef mural was a masterpiece, showing off every bit of sea life imaginable. The vivid hues of the knobby and patterned coral, tropical fish, and sparkling blue water called out to us and sparked our imagination. I had never been to a museum before, but gazing at this massive piece of art was breathtaking. If you are one of those people who are emotionally moved by art or music, as I am, you can understand my awe.

Our class also looked forward to the times when Mrs. Perenboom would read adventurous tales to us from books. The best part was when she would instruct us to lay our heads on our desks, close our eyes, and rest while she read aloud to us. I was being introduced to beauty, stillness, relaxation, and creativity.

While my brain didn't comprehend what was happening, my imagination and my soul certainly did. Art is good for our health, and Mrs. Perenboom knew that. She was introducing beauty and slow living to us on a daily basis through chalk art murals, tales of adventure, and good ole naps.

The American Congress of Rehabilitation Medicine claims that simply observing art can positively affect our health! "These benefits don't just come from making art, they also occur by experiencing art. Observing art can stimulate the creation of new neural pathways and ways of thinking." I believe my creativity was formed and solidified that year.

You may not be interested in scuba diving, or the art of watercolor painting, or the craft of creative writing. But even if you haven't found it yet, know that there is something inside of you that longs to create. Creativity can feel vulnerable, especially if you are a perfectionist, but it also gives us that needed fresh start if we slow down to welcome it. I wonder if we'll let ourselves shift from being in our own world of thoughts and problems to pausing in awe more often, as we let all manner of beauty awaken and change us.

For Reflection and Discussion

What are your thoughts as you contemplate the Bible verse about being a masterpiece (Ephesians 2:10)? Is it then freeing to know that you are also a work in progress?

If these last few years slowed you down, did you begin a new creative hobby or start dabbling in something that made you feel alive again? What was that?

Write a poem about yourself from the perspective of God as he saw you when he created you.

BENEDICTION

In this season of pause
With waves crashing
all around you
May you lament what
has been lost
And rejoice over new mercies
While holding hands
open in absolute hope.

Learning to Slow Down

Slow living is all about creating time and space and energy for the things that matter most to us in life, so ask yourself what you stand to gain.

BROOKE MCALARY

7

Rhythms for Sunrise to Sunset

*Set expectations for yourself that are not based on
what you believe everyone else is doing.*

JULIE HAGE

THERE ARE ALWAYS MILE MARKERS on the path, if we
only take the time to see them. On Bonaire, there are over fifty
oval stones, painted bright yellow, nestled in various locations,
telling drivers that they have arrived at a popular scuba diving
spot. A popular dive stop on the island is marked by a yellow
rock with the words "1000 Steps." This enormous staircase
built into the cliff takes the tourist from the paved road on its
curving steps, down to the rocky shoreline, and then out into
the reef.

If you are a tourist, each step gets you closer to the whole
reason you probably flew several thousand miles—to enjoy one of
the best underwater sanctuaries in the world. Similarly, each small
step in this invitation to slower living gets you closer to the life you
really want, where your yes means you can be an active participant
in your colorful life instead of a distant, weary observer.

Martin Luther King Jr. said, "Take the first step in faith. You
don't have to see the whole staircase, just take the first step."

This chapter will highlight some ways you can build in rhythms for starting and ending your day, one step at a time. See these rhythms as those painted yellow mile markers. Let them replace any overwhelm as they point out the predictable patterns you'd like to implement into your morning, afternoon, and evening. And remember, this needs to work for you. You don't have to do what you think others are doing if their rhythms cause you to hold your breath more than giving you reason to exhale.

Setting a rhythm is more about predictable patterns that are sustainable than about sticking to a schedule.

Setting a rhythm is more about predictable patterns that are sustainable than about sticking to a schedule.

I use the word *cozy* to start and end my own routine because it suggests being held by God. Like a chick nestling under the wings of the mama hen, feeling safe and seen by our Creator is grounding, especially when we have a hard day ahead, are afraid of unknowns unfolding, or are afraid to go to sleep at night.

On the island, it's easy to engage in slow living activities. Whether you are at the beach, under a palm tree, watching the flamingos, inspecting the cactus fence framing a dirt road, or windsurfing, there is a world of relaxation at your door. But we don't have to be on vacation to enjoy this feeling. Enjoying nature, whether that's sand or snow, is fundamental to finding our way back to an unhurried and connected life with those we love. Taking a brisk walk in the fresh cool air or sitting on the deck at the lake offers you a stillness that brings delight and peace.

Rest is a bigger deal than we think. Recharging is critical to not only our health, but also in the way we hear people. (If I have not had solid sleep, I am more irritable, and it's easier for me to misunderstand someone's comment or question.) Naps are underrated. Our island had siesta time from noon to two o'clock each weekday. Almost all retail shops, including the bank and places to pay utility bills, would close for lunch and rest. I remember many days when I saw my dad stretch out and take a nap on the carpet.

Slow Living Shift
Sustainable Rhythms

A shift to slow living doesn't necessarily mean your end goal is to sleep in your hammock all day with a piña colada nearby, although I'm sure there are a handful of people who might eagerly do that. It is an often-revisited season when you exhale and solidify what matters most to you in this life you have—soaking up the good and the excitement while not resenting the beautifully hard and mundane. When we pause to reflect and move forward, we begin to understand that the good and the hard parts of life hold hands. When the striving stops and your body slows down, the mind and heart can lean into a much better posture of listening—listening to yourself, to God, and to others. Being present to each day, holding our hands open and letting life unfold without manipulating and planning every moment, has a way of resetting our inner world. We take the pressure off ourselves when we focus more on everyday rhythms that feel sustainable or patterns that are simple and predictable, rather than get overwhelmed with tight schedules and unrealistic goals.

The freedom of discovering and then choosing what is most important to us is priceless. I was reminded during the Great Pause of 2020 that we do best when we can lift our gaze, see the world and people around us, and ask where we want to participate. Slowing down gives us a chance to be authentic in our life choices and desires.

It's so easy to be influenced by others. Saying no to what gurus or experts tell you is "the thing" to do simply gives you agency and a chance to find out what you really like. I don't like to go for a run or a jog in the morning. Or anytime, actually. I'd rather sit on my back patio! My friend Melanie has been told that she shouldn't have any dairy whatsoever. So, while she does limit it, she has figured out that she can occasionally enjoy a slice of cheese on a burger or a chocolate truffle instead of giving up all dairy—which is what she's really wanted. I think you know what you want too.

Slowing down gives us options and possibilities that not only boost our confidence but help solidify who we really are and what rhythms we might naturally move to.

For guidance in creating some of these predictable patterns, here are three easy rhythms I use on most days that span from early morning to when I go to sleep at night.

A Simple, Cozy Morning Rhythm

This is a framework to ensure you are all set to have a sweet time of solitude to start your day. Instead of dreading getting out of bed, or rushing around in a frenzy, a slow steady start to the day sets you up to feel like you gave your body and mind time to acclimate. These mini-rhythms are simple and doable and will infuse you with a fresh wind on a day where you may feel too tired and un-motivated to hit the ground running.

Here's your guide to setting up your simple, cozy morning:

1. Bring your tea, coffee, blanket, or heat pack to a cozy chair near a window. If my minutes of solitude are around sunrise, I like to pick a chair with a view of the eastern sky. Lingering with a hot beverage while the light changes is a beautiful way to usher in the new day. I also get my coffeepot or Keurig "almost ready" the night before. Personally, I love using Keurig tea pods for hot tea instead of having a kettle going. I also like to have a blanket nearby to throw over me for those colder mornings in my comfy chair.

2. Pick an activity for each day of the week from the following list or from your own ideas:

- Use the Daily Office for a short but fixed time of silence, prayer, and contemplation.
- Listen to a short podcast, audiobook, or Scripture reading plan.
- Read the current book you are in the middle of or the one on your to-be-read pile.
- Write your weekly to-do list, a grocery list, your novel, your prayer list, or a poem.
- Brainstorm a project or come up with that Easter or Thanksgiving menu.
- Dream about the future—mind map your spring garden, plan a fun trip for next year, or be curious about what that retirement plan could look like.
- Record a message in your phone's notes, leaving yourself some thoughts about your longings and creativity that you've buried deep inside of you.

- Being prepared the night before is key. If you have a basket or tray, fill it with items you would like to have with you. It might be a crossword puzzle, book, pen, journal, iPad, workbook, or clipboard with lined paper. Ask yourself what you want to do.

3. Set your phone's timer for twenty minutes and go place it across the room. We can't always be on island time! This act helps you stay within your intended timeframe and cuts out being distracted by a notification coming in. I have a habit of scrolling when my mind is not settled, so to eliminate the lure of the scroll, I put my phone out of sight at least ten feet away from me. Cellphones can be a big roadblock in the construction of new rhythms.

I have observed that daily devotions can be challenging for many people. It is for me some days. The spiritual life ebbs and flows over the years and some years are harder than ever. If you're a young mom, your arms may be full and your eyelids may be droopy. If you are past retirement age, your health concerns might be keeping you from things that used to be easy or routine. Please give yourself grace in all seasons. You are in a relationship with time; you are not working against it.

Will there be days when you need to change the scenery? Absolutely. This beautiful rhythm of slowing down to be present with God can happen anywhere. Be open to the Holy Spirit's invitation. Move outside and meet God on a walk, while fishing, or wherever your senses come alive and point you to the glory of God.

4. Silence, prayer, and settling in. Relax in silence for a minute. Spend another minute or two in prayer.

Ask God to be near, to guide your steps and to provide what you need just for today. Thank him for new morning mercies, fresh every day. Afterward, take a deep breath.

Now you are ready to settle in to either listen, read, write, brainstorm, or dream from whatever activity you picked earlier in number two. You are about to just *be*. This is important to not miss as it comes before the *do* part—the rest of your daily obligations that are waiting for you. Enjoy your quiet time and let it be what it is. Accepting that we cannot control the outcome of everything, especially how our day may unfold, brings a new level of acceptance and resolve. We will do our best and leave the desire for a results-oriented morning to the boardroom. Some things we will finish, and other things we will leave undone.

The Rhythm of Daily Office Hours

The word *office* shares a root with the Latin word *opus*, meaning "work," and the practice of fixed times of prayer throughout the day was named the "work of God" (*Opus Dei*) early in Christian tradition. This ancient spiritual discipline helps us stop in our day to be with God. At its simplest, it contains a morning or midday office followed by a midday or evening office. This can be broken down for five to twenty minutes each time. It is not a traditional quiet time or even Bible reading time. It is a sacred rhythm and routine, and most certainly not a task to be done or a box to be checked off. This practice reminds us to stop several times a day to listen to God, to be with God, and to take a breather with our Creator. Slowing down to do this helps to create and then solidify an awareness and deeper acquaintance with the Almighty.

My favorite book to use for this very purpose was written by author and pastor Peter Scazzero. It's called *Emotionally Healthy Spirituality Day by Day: A 40-Day Journey with the Daily Office.* I was thrilled to learn that this practice was the foundation for

God's people in the Bible. Scazzero points out that King David practiced set prayers seven times a day, Daniel prayed three times a day, and Jesus' own disciples after his death and resurrection continued to pray at fixed hours of the day.

Scazzero's Daily Office rhythm is set up in an easy and repetitive way: two minutes of silence and stillness, a short Scripture reading already printed out, a short devotional followed by a question for your consideration, a prayer you can read out loud, concluding with two minutes of silence to bring your time with God to a close.

While you can certainly use this in the morning, I like to use the Daily Office in the afternoon as a centering point. This rhythm helps me to once again slow down, exhale, and pause to rest with God for a bit. I love to have my afternoon coffee or tea at this time as well. Refreshment can come in many forms, so think about what a predictable pattern might be for you personally. Playing music? An afternoon walk?

* * *

I will leave all of the logistics of your nighttime routine up to you, as you know yourself best, so below is just a glimpse of the last thing I do as I get ready to turn in for the night. I simply repeat steps one through four from my Simple Cozy Morning Rhythm, to tell my mind and body that I'm heading for the land of solitude again.

My Simple Cozy Evening Rhythm

I warm up my heated eye mask in the microwave then throw it under the covers as I get ready for bed. I put a warm drink I've just prepared on my nightstand and set up my pillows so that I can sit up in bed for about twenty minutes.

I usually read on my Kindle or in a book to wind down for the evening. If I have not been on electronics much that day, then I indulge in a game of DuoTriGordle, which is a thirty-two-section Wordle game.

I will glance at my phone, but I'm not a stickler for ending my reading or game on time because I like to have natural endings, not forced endings. Remember as a kid having to leave the house for an evening obligation without finishing your TV show? No closure there.

I turn out the lights, do some deep inhaling and exhaling, literally sighing off the weariness of the day from my shoulders, back, and legs. I learned this from my mother and am so grateful to be able to copy her practice. I talk to God silently as my body and mind settle in for sleep. I am grateful for living yet another day.

The key to rhythms is not to force them or hold on so tightly that you feel guilt or shame when you miss one. Refreshing our hearts and minds looks different for everyone. If you need to feel the wind at your back or hear the birds in the trees to feel closer to God, then being in nature at sunrise, midday, or sunset is the perfect time to be quiet and have a contemplative stance. That's your quiet time with God, in the most literal sense of the word. At the end of the day, the human heart will always long for a taste of relationship versus a list of quiet-time checkboxes.

> *At the end of the day, the human heart will always long for a taste of relationship versus a list of quiet-time checkboxes.*

For Reflection and Discussion

How might steady yet gentle rhythms help you better than a tight schedule or rigid requirements?

Which routine is easier—morning or evening? Does it bother you to leave things undone or is it freeing to just let them go?

Do you have a favorite ritual or sustaining rhythm to start or end your day that works well for you?

8

Soul Care for a Slowed-Down Life

The world has gone and got itself in an awful rush,
to whose benefit I do not know. We are too busy
for our own good. We need to slow down.
Our lifestyles are destroying us. The worst
part is, we are rushing east in search of a sunset.

MATTHEW KELLY

SUSTAINABLE RHYTHMS are natural and important parts of starting and ending our day. But soul care is the foundation of slow living. It is the piece everything else is built on. A sturdy base, if you will, for all aspects of a slower lifestyle. We are spiritual beings who have physical and emotional needs. I have read much about self-care over the years and certainly acknowledge its importance, but I believe it comes after we have fully implemented *soul care*. Like the gentle lapping of the incoming waves on the shore, we, too, can have gentle ways of implementing soul care and its sister, self-care.

Spiritual practices are the beams that rise up from the foundation of our intentional soul care work, supporting the rooftop

Spiritual practices are the beams that rise up from the foundation of our intentional soul care work, supporting the rooftop where we lounge with God.

where we lounge with God. Such practices, also known as spiritual disciplines, are ancient or modern activities repeated regularly for the purpose of spiritual development and cultivating a closer life with God. While there are many wonderful spiritual practices, thankfully, we don't have to race to complete all of them or aim to get a gold star! In this chapter, I am sharing a few that have greatly impacted my shift to slow living instead of focusing on ones you may already be doing—like prayer, worship, reading Scriptures, lectio divina, or meditation.

Slow Living Shift
Soul Care Practices

David Mathis, author of *Habits of Grace*, says it best: "The final joy in any truly Christian discipline or practice or rhythm of life is, in the words of the apostle, 'the surpassing worth of knowing Christ Jesus my Lord.'" Here, Mathis is referring to the apostle Paul's words in Philippians 3:8, which Paul penned while in prison. May we know Jesus better through deep soul care—our spiritual disciplines.

Spiritual Direction: A Practice of Noticing What God Is Inviting You To

Spiritual direction, a very old practice, is returning as a wonderful option for anyone who would like to process their ordinary life with God with the guidance of another person trained in this field. A good spiritual director will not tell you how to think or what to do in a difficult situation. Spiritual direction is not therapy, mentoring, or even pastoral counseling. A good explanation of what spiritual direction is comes from spiritual director Emily P. Freeman, who says:

> Spiritual direction is a counter-cultural practice of co-listening for anyone who wants to deepen their awareness of and relationship with God. It allows space for curiosity, discovery, and held silence. It's a space where both people submit to the movement of God and where one person listens without an agenda.

I have observed these qualities in Maeve, my own spiritual director: she has empathy, kindness, understanding, humility, patience, is not afraid of silence, and has a rich prayer life. Maeve's biggest gift to me, however, is listening.

I like to envision three chairs present in a spiritual direction session. One for the guide, one for the directee, and one for God. Matthew 18:20 (KJV) says, "For where two or three are gathered together in my name, there am I in the midst of them." I wonder why the word *gather* was chosen as opposed to the words *praying, talking, fellowshipping,* or *walking.* Could it be that it's all encompassed in this setting, perhaps?

Sometimes we need someone who is present with us, listening to our unfolding and searching, but instead of giving advice or answers, they are listening for ways to explain back to us what our words may not be able to name. My direction sessions are always a precious time of clarity, a rhythm of paying attention to my inner life as another believer comes alongside me. Maeve helps me be present and notice God's movement in my life. She holds space for my questions and comments as we both listen, reflect, and discern. She always asks what I sense God inviting me to.

I used to be uncomfortable with awkward silence, but I have come to feel secure with the occasional pause, sigh, or lull. It is a rare and much-needed space to process and make room for the Holy Spirit to work. Sometimes our hearts need a minute to just be as we gather our thoughts and words. Sometimes ideas or clarity form a week or two after a session with Maeve. She not only primes the pump of the well in my soul, but also sets the table for a future gathering. Her hospitality and contemplation guide me as I go about my life and meet with God on my own.

She always asks what I sense God inviting me to.

Spiritual direction with Maeve has helped me slow down to practice what I call "barefoot hospitality." While we have to be hospitable to ourselves before we can fully welcome others, we also need to know that God welcomes us to be with him—in the same way he welcomed little, barefoot children who came to him.

Barefoot hospitality encompasses the practices you engage in by yourself and then with others as you move toward a deeper relationship with God. Below are a few of my favorite soul care practices to use in addition to spiritual direction.

Breath Prayer: A Practice for When You Are Anxious

While I look forward to hearing sermons, praying with friends, studying the Bible, and meeting with my spiritual director once a month, not all of our practices are easy and fluid. Sometimes it's good to have something in our pocket for times when we are all alone or are highly anxious about what may hit us. This is where a practice known as breath prayer fits in. It's an invisible support beam, increasing trust and reliance on God in fearful times.

Breath prayer is the merging of a powerful tool to manage anxiety with an ancient Christian practice rooted in Scripture. We already know that deep, slow breathing calms the body. No part of our body is autonomous. Deep breathing encourages our central nervous system to slow down, which in turn affects the area of the brain where tension, trauma, and nervousness reside, inviting our nervous system to come back to the present. This practice is short and repetitive, and can be done anywhere:

1. Choose a verse or two of Scripture with a natural halfway point. Breathe in while considering the first half of the text.

2. Breathe out with the second half of the text.

Jennifer Tucker, author of *Breath as Prayer: Calm Your Anxiety, Focus Your Mind and Renew Your Soul,* is a favorite writer and illustrator of mine. Her book came out of her own experiences of finding breath prayer as a lifeline while her daughter was in the hospital. It was here that the Holy Spirit prompted Jenn to breathe and pray the words, "The Lord is my shepherd; I have all that I need" to calm her own anxiety. Jenn writes, "That simple prayer helped quiet my worries and fears. The deep breathing helped to calm the physical symptoms of my anxiety, and the prayer helped me to recenter my thoughts on Christ and His love for me, and I drifted off to sleep with a renewed peace."

Photojournalism: A Practice for When You Don't Have the Words

Some days, when the words don't come as easily, I find myself grabbing my phone or camera and heading to the backyard or down the street. I'm wanting to meet God in the beauty of my surroundings, whatever season that might happen to be in. It's not hard to do when our whole world is an invitation to slow down. Photojournalism is simply documenting your surroundings or a particular object; the details of the scene can tell the story without words.

When we capture the image of a snowflake resting on a step, a butterfly in flight, or the pink and orange hues of a sunset in the distance, we slow down to take in the majesty and glory of our Creator. Images take the place of words to spell out what our souls are seeing. Whether you do anything with that image or not is up to you. You might want to share it with a friend, post it for the world to see, or simply keep it as a quiet reminder of the gift in that moment.

I recall a particularly tough day when I couldn't come up with a written paragraph for my peer writing group. Instead of sitting at my desk in disappointment, I walked outside with my dog and looked up to see purple wisteria adorning the foliage near our old shed. I snapped a few pictures, capturing the magnificent details of the flowering beauty. While I couldn't write anything for a few more days, the words came tumbling out later that week after I spent some time admiring those details in my photographs.

Photojournalism should be mentally and physically relaxing. It isn't scrapbooking. Many times, words don't even accompany the photo. It is not forcing a scene or picking the absolute best picture out of twenty. Sometimes (surprise!) it may even be best just to observe without documenting.

As I am writing this section, it's almost golden hour. A few minutes ago, my teen daughter walked over and alerted me to the incredible pink and orange streaks in the sky outside of the sunroom windows to the west. As I oohed and aahed and mumbled that I couldn't find my phone to grab a picture, she paused and said, "Mom, what if we just watch it together instead?" And the irony is not lost on me.

What started out as pink cotton candy skies morphed into peach delight before ending as a fiery orange display—something I would have missed had I been trying to get the perfect shot. But our cameras can help us. When we take a picture, we slow the moment by freezing it in place. Being present to life means pausing and being in the moment, taking in the breathtaking beauty of God's creation. Who we were with and the fact that we chose to pause in that scene solidifies the value of slowing down. It's all worth remembering and thanking God for. You only need your camera or cellphone to unhurry and enjoy this spiritual practice.

Spiritual Friendship: A Practice of Gathering in Person

This practice centers around gathering with others who are like-minded in the faith, not necessarily in the same denomination. Presence with others in person matters, even while much of our daily interaction can be online. Perhaps that is sharing a deep conversation about what God is doing in your life over a cup of coffee with a neighbor, or attending a weekly or monthly time of Scripture study and prayer; you can decide what fits your heart the best. Seek these times of holding both delight and lament, of being seen and heard, for both you and the other person involved. Our faces reflect to one another; we are truly seen and see each other.

This is not corporate worship or a special event with music and some preaching. This is intentional time with another person or very small group of people. Spiritual intimacy cannot happen in a large crowd. Iron sharpening iron cannot be beneficial if there is no relationship to draw on, including privacy, trust, and space. Fellowship in community is important in spiritual growth. It's what I call #communityforyoursoul because it nourishes us as the Trinity always intended. We need each other more these days than ever, but without slowing down to be intentional, even with just a few people, it's awfully hard to make that a reality.

An idea of what this might look like for you could be simply joining an established life group from your church. It may be necessary for you to find a faith-based community in your town or start one yourself with a few people. Another possibility is to ask your church administrator if there is a church member who is housebound but would like fellowship to come to them on occasion. People in this situation can always watch a sermon online, but that does not take the place of the true in-person fellowship that almost everyone longs for, especially those with chronic and invisible illnesses, mothers with new babies, and the elderly.

* * *

Soul care is more about engaging with God than about taking specific actions. I pray that as you pursue soul care in new and meaningful ways, some of these spiritual practices will be beneficial and produce much growth in your Christian journey. While they are intended to match well with the shift you are making to a slower, more intentional life, may they also lead you toward much joy and closeness in your personal walk with God.

For Reflection and Discussion

What do you think of when you imagine lounging with God on a rooftop? It's very similar to relaxing with friends on a porch or rooftop deck.

Think about which of the soul care practices you'll try.

9

Where's Your Island in the City?

*We who live in quiet places have the opportunity
to become acquainted with ourselves, to think our
own thoughts and live our own lives in a way that
is not possible for those keeping up with the crowd.*

LAURA INGALLS WILDER

WHEN I WAS A TEENAGER, our house on the south end of the island was perched on a small cliff, overlooking the white sand and the turquoise waters. The sea was so clear that you could see the reef from the house. Often, when I wanted to be alone, I would throw on my floral swimsuit, walk through the dusty backyard, and head backward down the old, rusty steel ladder anchored into the cliff.

As my feet hit the hot sand, little crabs would scurry, and my heart would swell with the knowledge that I would soon be transported to a different world. Never mind the fact that I was already on a desolate little island in the Caribbean.

I would swim out to a bright yellow circular raft that our neighbor Tex (from Las Vegas) had anchored in the sandy bottom outside of the reef. I would hoist myself up onto this raft—sometimes like a mermaid, but usually like a seal. Naturally, the rhythm of the lapping water and the sun-warmed plastic on my skin lulled me into a slower pace. Letting all the water droplets keep me cool, I would stretch out to relax on that yellow piece of plastic paradise, with my face toward the horizon.

As far as my eyes could take me, there was only the sea. We were fifty miles north of the Venezuelan coast. When the horizon goes on forever, you feel like a lonely little dot in the world. At least that's what I would have been if I'd zoomed out on Google Maps.

Some days while reef lounging, I would just close my eyes and wonder what the rest of the world was up to . . . people in other countries, other communities, other islands. On other trips to the yellow raft, my eyes would follow the rainbow-colored parrot fish swimming underneath me. The coral shapes were intriguing. I would both taste and smell the salty air. I would hear the swishing of the lone palm tree or banana tree up in the yard above.

A Deeper Experience

I didn't even realize that this time alone with my thoughts, and alone with God, was the beginning of my own journey of spiritual formation: practicing solitude, stillness, and listening. In fact, I didn't even understand the words "spiritual formation" until a few years ago. But we have a steadfast God, who is gracious to pursue us our entire lives and to walk alongside us in this journey of learning what it's like to be more like Christ.

Many of us don't take advantage of the beauty of stillness in creation to ease anxiety, but desire for it is woven into the very fabric of our being. It's tangible and meant for our enjoyment. It's ours for the taking with our five senses. We are all looking for a deeper experience with God whether we know it or not.

And these experiences we have meeting with God in a quiet place are foundational and formational. They aren't meant to be experienced only once. They help shape who we are, our attachment to God, and how we share that experience with others in our life. Personally, I am so grateful to go back in time and pull a memory back out, just as I am also thankful to create a safe new memory in a new place.

Slow Living Shift
Finding Sanctuary

If you haven't already, I encourage you to find your island in the city. This will be a tool that you can use practically anywhere and in any situation in which you need to calm your anxiety and feel more tethered to God. Your secret place of reef lounging, your oasis—whether it's in your mind or in a physical location. A lovely place where just you and God can meet in silence. A place to enjoy the unhurried pace of the moment for however long or short that may be. Let this place be special, safe, and cozy if that is what you need.

We all need a sanctuary.

The word *sanctuary* came to us through French from Latin, and blends the meanings of a *safe* place and a *holy* place. What a beautiful way to think of God being with us in the stillness. Many women I talk with say that their sanctuary (or island in the city) is out on their front porch or in the old, comfy chair near the window in their bedroom. Where they hold their steaming mug of hot coffee mixed with

We all need a sanctuary.

their favorite creamer and savor the moment. Some people pray during this time. Some people settle their overwhelmed and anxious hearts here in their space of quiet and private serenity.

But no matter where you are physically, you can return in memory to a safe and holy location, either simple or complex. If you crave extreme beauty out in nature as your place, take some time to recall a tropical vacation spot, a snow-covered mountain from a ski trip, or a waterfall in the rainforest. If you long for a quiet place of nostalgia, try the leather chair in your grandfather's library, where you linger in the scent of old books and the sweet aroma of his pipe. Maybe your aunt's farm, overflowing with bounty from the orchards, is your sanctuary to go back to.

Let this time and place be the remedy to your weariness in this hard season.

Being still, being out in nature, and being quiet are important ways we can take care of our soul and hear God speak to us. If you live in a busy city and walk to work, is there a little refuge that you might possibly pass by? Is there a quaint rose garden tucked onto a section of a street perhaps? Maybe an old bench is sitting nearby? If you sat there for a few minutes each day, what would that feel like? Seeing the beauty of the roses, smelling the floral goodness of life?

Your soul care sanctuary will most likely be an actual place, full of tangible things like a blanket, a coffee cup, plants, and seashells. But sometimes we must return to places in our mind if we can't physically get there. On days where I need to breathe in deeply, I sometimes go back in my memory to that yellow raft. Our senses mixing with our memories are amazing. Being transported back to a beautiful place can calm the nervous system and help us appreciate our surroundings. This is also an arrow to contentment and gratitude if we'll follow it.

"Reef lounging" could be the phrase you use for this slow living method. Whatever fits best with your personality! Like slipping into a fresh pool of water, we can ease into a quiet space with God where we are still and where we can listen or where we can find refuge and receive his peace.

Don't be afraid of the stillness you are craving. It will turn out to be life-giving in the most unexpected ways.

Psalm 46:10 says, "Be still, and know that I am God." This is an invitation to pause, reflect, and quiet our hearts, knowing we have help. While we are alone in this moment, we are never truly alone in this life. Hurry rushes us through life hoping we will forget the very things that anchored us in the first place. Don't be afraid of the stillness you are craving. It will turn out to be life-giving in the most unexpected ways.

Where Others Find Sanctuary

Here are some examples from my friends of their own specific soul care sanctuaries. I think you'll be comforted by the simplicity of their locations and surroundings. My hope is that maybe these descriptions will give you an idea of practical and personal places you can go reef lounging when you need to let God tend to your soul.

Kate has a place where she goes reef lounging in her mind. It's in the Olympic Mountains, a gorgeous location on the Quinault River in the state of Washington. She goes back to the river spot where she and her father would take trips to go fishing. Hearing the rapids, feeling the wind on her face, seeing the mountain peaks in the distance, and being with her father, who she has always adored, became much more than a fishing expedition. The beauty surrounding Kate and the connection to her father created this sanctuary that she could take home with her and pull out of her memory at a moment's notice. While she may not return as frequently or at all in the coming years, Kate will always have this memory she can pull up and sit with at any time, in any place. In recent years, Kate has brought her love of nature and beauty to the canvas. A new island in the city might just be her art room where she teaches watercolor painting. Or anywhere she can create art in silence.

Lissa found that the stillness in her car, traveling the North Carolina roads, between visiting hospice patients, is where she does her best reef lounging most weeks. She holds a heavy service of care to humankind, as she sits with both patients and family members in their pain. Lissa administers love and relief to the patient in front of her as she carries out the decency of walking someone home. Even the strongest people, empowered with the skills and personality to help people in their darkest days, need a quiet respite of their own. And while Lissa's quiet electric car is where she recharges and reflects, these days her screened-in back porch has also become her sanctuary.

Chris works from home and says his sanctuary in his busy residence is his office—simply because there is a door. This feels relatable!

Nicole says that her island in the city is one of the beaches in Connecticut where she, her husband, and children go to walk, find shells, and discover sea glass nestled in the sand. Away from the busyness of writing, seeing her therapy clients, and packing lunches, Nicole savors her slow and steady walks. With her head down, she intently searches for beauty to bring her into a place of relaxation and stillness with God.

My husband Dean has a recycled greenhouse in our backyard that is often his island in the city. This is where he prepares seedlings to eventually go into garden boxes and mixes soil and nutrients in buckets. It's a quiet location to dehydrate and grind bunches of red-hot peppers into flakes for bottled gifts to bestow on his coworkers. Dean has also been known to roast the Thanksgiving turkey out in the greenhouse instead of in the busy and crowded kitchen. That's some calm meal prep right there!

If you resist being still, movement like a brisk run in the evening or dancing when no one is at home may be where you do your best reef lounging, feeling free to express yourself and commune with your Creator. Or if you are weary, maybe it looks like snuggling in bed with your puppy and lots of blankets.

These days, as I sit in our retro bungalow off Main Street, this home has surely become my island in the city. The sunroom, with its nine windows, mismatched chairs, and quirky island decor, is my sanctuary from the busyness of life. Our three cats seem to feel the same way. I'll frequently turn from my desk to see them napping in here with me, almost every day. Our quiet street helps me feel anchored and settled—my own version of reef lounging.

While I spent sixteen formative years on the island, I may retire here in our quaint house in town. If so, the years will go by with me riding my beach cruiser under these 120-year-old oak trees that canopy our street. Sure, it's not the same as an island in the Caribbean, but our ordinary days make up most of our lives.

These collective moments are beautiful. Birds and the occasional train whistle will call out to me, instead of the salty sea lulling me with its warm embrace. And while I can go reef lounging in the turquoise sea at any time in my mind, being outside and spying on our neighbor's gorgeous cream-colored magnolias might also give my soul the space it needs to breathe.

I had to escape to my "island in the city" a while back during an MRI I was dreading. With some relaxing essential oils to smell, reggae music in my ears, and my head hanging out of the metal cylinder, I imagined I was back on that yellow raft, doing some reef lounging. It did help that this medical facility had decided to put a palm-leaf decal on the ceiling above the MRI machine. But there I was, back to magically feeling the sun on my face, the wind in my hair, and watching the sea shining like diamonds—right there in a big building. I used this technique the other day at the dentist with success! While it didn't work as well for my mammogram screening or while I was sliding around in the back of a police cruiser, it's undoubtedly a simple way to calm your mind and heart for a bit.

For Reflection and Discussion

Think about what it feels like or will feel like to meet with God in silence in a safe place. Describe your feeling of communing with God there.

Are you afraid of the stillness your soul may be craving, or are you expectant? Recall when your own journey of spiritual formation began.

Take a moment to list a few places that come to mind for you where you can go reef lounging in your mind. Also list places that are your soul care sanctuary in your current surroundings at home or in your town. Keep this list in your back pocket, so to speak, and pull it out whenever you need it.

10

Savoring, One Sip at a Time

Don't slide through life. Savor it. Slow down,
be kind, pay attention. Because this isn't going
to happen again.

Carrie Fisher

Sometimes the late afternoon sunset hits just
right on a beach vacation. It's the perfect indication that the day
is coming to an end. A breeze gently touches sunburned skin.
Freshly washed hair begins to blow dry as you anchor into your
chaise longue out on the wide balcony. The beach below looks
stark, long emptied of its brightly colored umbrellas, towels, and
scurrying children.

Supper is passed around on paper plates. Music starts to drift
by more frequently and friends start settling deeper into conversation. As the stars start to arrive on the scene, like tiny twinkle
lights strung across a vast navy-blue sky, you can feel your body
relax in a way it never does at work, in class, while commuting, or
even at church. The clinking of glasses, the pounding of waves,
the swishing of palm fronds nearby invites you to slow down even
more. An intentional savoring begins at some point, usually un-
noticed, and is enjoyed over and over again, one sip at a time.

I have enjoyed several of these vacations at our friend Kevin's beachfront condo. One of my favorite ways to relax is to sit around this balcony table with friends, eating dinner and sipping on a drink. Some of these trips have been with my girlfriends or with my husband and daughter. Each trip has included untold hours facing the sea.

Have you ever been on a cruise or noticed a colorful flier from a travel agency? Nothing quite says "slow down and savor" like one of those tiny, colorful paper drink umbrellas that are wedged into a piece of fruit that's nestled in a tropical drink. These parasols are such happy little trinkets, symbols of relaxation and refreshment that are meant to be savored. Enjoying a festive piña colada while lounging in a beach chair sounds good, and we can all envision it, but this practice doesn't have to be saved for a vacation or cruise.

Slow Living Shift
Savoring

I hope you are relishing in the fact that the slow living practice for this chapter is *savoring*. I can't wait to hear how it impacts and benefits your intention of slowing down.

Nourishing our body and soul are key to not only a slower and more intentional life, but a life lived at a sustainable and enjoyable pace. One step at a time and one sip at a time. When you do something slowly because you want the moment, experience, or feeling to last forever, that's a fine way of savoring:

- nibbling on a good piece of chocolate
- smelling the bloom of a honeysuckle
- soaking in a hot bath, the warm water enveloping you
- standing out in the misty rain after a hot spell
- enjoying snuggling the sleeping baby in your arms

We can also savor challenging and sorrowful moments, which is a way of honoring a person or experience. In making a moment last with a loved one, we are slowing down time at the bedside of one who is about to take their last breath. Savoring is the key that keeps us present in the moment. We honor each other in this way.

Our family doesn't go out to eat very often (unless you count Jersey Mike's subs). But one thing we have started is a new tradition of having dinner at a four-star restaurant the week after Christmas. It's the one time when I don't want the meal to end. I cannot pronounce some things on the menu, like *foie gras* or *haricots verts*, but the staff makes sure we are able to savor all five courses. We linger over each plate, slowly enjoying the delicacies that are spaced far apart. You cannot be in a hurry if you eat here, as everything is made fresh by the sous and pastry chefs.

God may not grace our laps with white linen napkins, but he does set a table before us in the presence of our enemies. Fear, suffering, and loneliness will hit us at inopportune times, but savoring God's goodness in our lives and having a place card with our name on it at his table are things we can count on continually.

A Fear of Missing Out

FOMO. I want to do all the things—and this feeling has been a kink in my slow living rule of life. But what if we know there is enough? Enough joy, enough laughter, enough togetherness. We are not late to our own life. But there's a tension between wondering if we're missing something good and feeling expectant. Dr. Quantrilla Ard says:

Nothing is missing. I'm sitting in the both/and of it all. Keeping a positive outlook and taking small, but obedient steps. The changes have felt unbearable in the past, but when I realize that being at the Chef's table is the best place to savor the dining experience, peace envelops me. All the things I've been through have brought me to this very moment. I'm waiting with expectancy.

A favorite memory etched in my mind when I think of community and savoring would be afternoons spent at the airport restaurant and bar on Bonaire. The breeze would whoosh in through the open-air facility, highlighting the ease of life as visitors walked across the tarmac and came through the little customs line. This local eatery was my favorite place to order french fries because they were always greasy. My friends and I looked forward to dipping our hot fries in ramekins of peanut satay sauce.

I would savor my appetizer and watch the older men in the community play loud games of dominoes, while they told stories and rolled with laughter. The sound of bone tiles slamming down on the bar tables and the scent of those greasy french fries always filled the air. The occasional bird would hop into this open-air building, expecting to snatch up a lone crumb that had fallen on the tile floor. The brown Amstel and green Heineken glass beer bottles clinked like a windchime, right over the hum of conversation. When I was young, it felt like time would stand still here.

You may have also experienced something similar while traveling through places I have not been, like Italy, Portugal, or Brazil. Freelance writer Captain Tim says:

"El Domino" is for Puerto Ricans not simply a game of strategy or just a pastime, but also an activity around which community relationships are built and sustained. Around the domino table, the players & families interact—cooking, playing music together and just mingling; therefore dominoes become a social-familiar event, almost a ritual, in which all become refreshed and spiritually recharged.

We can learn a lot from people groups and communities who stop and take the time to savor experiences and relationships. Being present is the key.

Whether you are demolishing an ice cream cone on a hot summer day or cozying up by a warm fireplace, lingering in the little pleasures nourishes the soul and gives it the fuel to keep going in this harsh world. If the savoring happens when we are with friends, it becomes a shared experience, giving our senses a soulful high-five.

Is God on Island Time?

I will always recall attending a classmate's birthday party when I was about twelve. My mother pulled up at the designated pickup time, but unfortunately for me, the party had just begun and would go late into the night. When she had dropped me off earlier, I'd been the only child there for the first hour—everyone else was on "island time" but me. Celebrating our people, being present in the moment, lingering and enjoying food, music, laughter, and conversation, is something that locals knew how to do well.

What would happen if we understood that God is like a host at this party, welcoming people way past the time stamped on the invitation? He's glad to see us and naturally has all the time in the world for his children. Once we grasp this, it's so much easier to linger with others in the same way, savoring the laughter and the celebration.

That little yellow and pink umbrella in your drink is symbolic of our life rhythms and the joy we can experience by savoring the tiniest of things. My friend Sarah Westfall often talks about noticing the little things that make you smile. I call it ordinary soul care. Sarah calls it "liturgy of the little things."

God is like a host at this party, welcoming people way past the time stamped on the invitation.

We give up what could be good and satisfying times of connection with others more times than we realize because of our fast-paced society. Sometimes, like the extra footage shown after the movie credits roll in a Marvel sequel, we experience pockets of delight when we linger, savor, and leave room for the surprises.

My friend and author Prasanta Verma's beautiful words on community and feasting together bring me a smile.

As I walk along the mountains and valleys of this physical life, I know this much: I don't want to feast on this charcuterie alone, abundant with the sweet, sour, and savory, whether sumptuous or skimpy . . . I want the souls of others around me, feasting together in the buffet of this beauty-ravaged life. I know the joy of fullness, the ache of emptiness. The truth is, life is often both at once, servings of delight mixed with grief.

As I think of the Last Supper, when Jesus broke bread and had intimate conversations with his disciples, I am reminded that we are instructed to do likewise—an important part of maintaining a community of believers. Since Jesus was a carpenter as well as a one-time vintner and sommelier, I wonder what he would do if he lived in our time. Would he host meals on charcuterie boards made of Jerusalem pine or olive tree wood? While we can speculate, we do know that he took good care of people.

* * *

A rooted and nostalgic exercise is to construct a poem using the framework built by writer and teacher George Ella Lyon. The poem is called "I Am From." I'm sharing mine below. I encourage you to take a quiet moment to write your own I Am From poem, as you see the parts about yourself that make you uniquely you. Here are some things you can include:

- People: grandparents, parents, siblings, neighbors, teachers, friends
- Food: tastes and smells, candy from the drugstore, apples from the orchard, fish from the pond, eggs from the farmer's chickens, homemade key lime pie at Grandma's, a cool Pepsi on a porch swing, Sunday dinners, hot cocoa on the ski trip, frozen treats from the ice cream truck
- Entertainment: the neighborhood pool, music from your era, movies at the drive-in, cartoons on a Saturday morning, crossword puzzles in the newspaper with breakfast, songs played at the ballpark or theater

- Places you've visited: a church pew, the merry-go-round, Disney World, the beach dunes, a dusty country road, your tire swing, your cafeteria.

Some thoughts will bring either a smile or a scowl to your face. Or you may wish you had a different answer to fill in. Part of shifting our perception on life, and accepting who we have become as the years have gone by, comes from savoring memories, places, and the timelines that make up our one, precious life. If you want a completely positive spin on your poem, just write it from an optimistic perspective, which is also what we do when we savor the moment.

I AM FROM

Jodi Grubbs

I am from peanut satay dip for french fries.

From windsurfing regattas to carnival parades.

I am from the house with the windows open, steel drum
band music wafting in like a lullaby from the hotel
across the street.

I am from cactus, palm trees, sea glass, and sea breeze.

I'm from languages mixed together to form community
and goodbyes on the tarmac under the hot sun.

From Oliver & Ida May and Melvin & Evelyn—although
an ocean and a lifetime away.

I am from missionary radio work and fried plantains with
homemade French Silk pie.

I am from Dutch stock, smooth wooden sandals, and tulips.

From the parents who always chose us kids over the ministry.

From the furloughs back and forth from sand to snow.

Old shells in boxes and retro photos in albums bring a
smile to my face.
Everyday island living finds me once again.

Pieces of our story are made up of moments that have been
savored by not only us, but generations before us. Some things
were chosen without our knowledge or consent. Some pieces are
whole, and many are broken. And we will hand down fragments
of pain and delight to our children and grandchildren, adding to
the narrative of our family tree.

As a young child, many Caribbean nights I fell asleep to the
rhythm of a steel drum band: a beautiful rhythm of slow drifting-
out-to-sea living. To this day, I can hear in my mind the tink-tink
sounds of the sticks hitting hollow drums, the melody reverber-
ating through the breezy night air. While I cannot recreate that
experience, I can reminisce and be grateful for the way it put me
to sleep as a girl.

My great-grandmother, who died just before she turned one
hundred, was known for gulping down her first morning cup of
coffee while it was scalding hot. But her second cup? She savored
that one, drinking it slowly, lingering for a spell in the strong flavor
and earthy smell.

Reverend Summer Gross, an Anglican priest and my soul
friend, reflected on savoring and our senses in a podcast episode
she hosted. She shares, "So often I spin through life caught in the
web of my self-made narrative. And I wonder. How often do I walk
the streets of my own life, eyes shut to the sweetness?" I hope to
not miss the sweetness.

The Elusive Green Flash

Routine moments from our growing-up years or our lives today are one thing to savor. But what about once-in-a-lifetime experiences? Perhaps there's something on your bucket list that you may only experience once, yet you hope to make the moment last and hold on to it for the precious, breathtaking gift it is.

Being a lover of oceans and sunsets, seeing the elusive "green flash" was one of those goals for me! It requires patience, stillness, and days of trying and trying again. This rare phenomenon occurs when the light of the sun touches the horizon. Reds, oranges, and yellows from that sunset or sunrise are absorbed into the atmosphere. Blue and violet light waves are then scattered, which leave behind a green light wave. This whole experience only lasts for two seconds. While often observed by sailors out to sea, I only managed to see it occur once in those sixteen years that I lived on the island. But once is really all I need in this lifetime.

We can get so frustrated when we have to hurry up and wait, but savoring helps us stay in the moment no matter how long or how short it is. Sometimes we forget to savor because our expectations are too high. Other times, we refuse to savor because we think we are missing out on something bigger and better, so we move on quickly, passing by the moment that was standing right in front of us, begging to be seen and valued. Patience is elusive when we think we will miss out.

Author Anne Morrow Lindbergh was an expert at savoring life. In her famous book *Gift From the Sea*, Lindbergh says:

> The sea does not reward those who are too anxious, too greedy, or too impatient. To dig for treasures shows not only impatience

and greed, but lack of faith. Patience, patience, patience, is what the sea teaches. Patience and faith. One should lie empty, open, choiceless as a beach—waiting for a gift from the sea.

When we savor our right-now life, instead of digging furiously for more exciting treasure, we can catch glimmers of beauty and taste and see God's goodness.

For Reflection and Discussion

What comes to mind when you think of savoring something?

Does knowing where you are from, like the I Am From poem, help you fit the pieces of your story together? How does it help you pause and savor now?

Consider writing your own version of this poem.

Reread the quote from Lindbergh's *Gift from the Sea*. Do you agree that patience is a big part of savoring?

11

Solitude and Spaciousness

*The more we train ourselves to spend time with God
and God alone, the more we will discover that God
is with us at all times and in all places. Then we will
be able to recognize God even in the midst of a busy
and active life. Once the solitude of time and space
has become a solitude of the heart, we will never
have to leave that solitude. We will be able to
live the spiritual life in any place.*

Henri J. M. Nouwen

IF YOU CAN REMEMBER a time when you were alone without being lonely, that was solitude.

This world is clamoring for our attention at every turn. The spiritual life is not full of multitasking or things to accomplish. Hearing God's still, small voice is almost impossible when the volume of life is turned up. Being alone with our thoughts in a quiet place helps to still our hearts and set the table for a feast of soul nourishment that only God can provide.

If you've ever wondered what solitude might feel like if you had a bird's-eye view from up high, my dad's friend Denny experienced this about once a week at work. Those missionary radio station towers on Bonaire were situated on the south end of the island so that broadcasts could reach 80 percent of the Western Hemisphere. Which meant that most of these steel towers were five hundred feet tall, with the biggest one towering at 670 feet in the air. Denny was one of the very few people who maintained these towers, and he would regularly climb to the top of one of them to inspect or fix it. He told me that he would often take advantage of the quiet space to eat his lunch in complete privacy while admiring the beauty of creation.

Denny said that sometimes he would be struck with total awe that God would use his childhood passions on the mission field. First climbing trees as a boy, then climbing telephone poles as a young man, and now ascending radio towers to further kingdom work. Although that kind of height terrifies me, I am a bit envious of the immense solitude that Denny had access to. Not to mention that bird's-eye view of paradise—from the turquoise sea, where he could see scuba divers walk into the water and disappear, to the blushing hues of the nearby briny lake across from the working salt flats glistening like white hills of ice. On occasion, Denny even saw the mountaintops of Venezuela, which are fifty miles south of our part of the Caribbean.

Me, the Wind, and God

As a teen, I rode past those huge salt flats and that pinkish water on many occasions. I would often explore the southern part of the island on my green bicycle, trying to spy flamingoes or the occasional piece of driftwood that resembled a piece of home decor. There were stretches where it was only me, the wind, and God. I didn't know at the time that I was practicing solitude. With each push of the pedal, I inhaled quiet refreshment—gravitating toward this spiritual practice without knowing its name. I simply knew that my soul was at rest, and it made me feel happy to be alone and free for a few hours. In the eighties, we had very little crime on the island, so my parents gave me quite a bit of freedom, which was a gift for my free-spirited self.

In those same teen years, my youth group would occasionally take advantage of the solitude and spaciousness of Klein Bonaire. This was a small, uninhabited island directly across from Bonaire, only accessible by boat or a very long swim. There is no electricity on this desolate island. Since there were no streetlights or city life surrounding us, our favorite thing to do in the pitch-black night, besides stargazing, was to play the old game of capture the flag on the sand and in the brush. It's truly suspenseful when you cannot see whether the person moving nearby is a foe or a friend. On Klein Bonaire sleepovers, the blackness was so rich and palpable that the stars could only shine brighter, sprinkling the heavens above like baby diamonds.

Solitude is the picnic blanket that is spread out on the landscape of our busy life, offering a safe place to stretch out and cloudgaze, alone with our thoughts in the big wide world.

Slow Living Shift
Seeking Out Solitude

Implementing solitude allows us to train ourselves to spend time with God so that we can better hear his voice. Alone, physically and mentally, with no one to bother you for a bit. The radio is off. Your phone is set to vibrate. This might look like a solitary stroll in your neighborhood or favorite park; or sitting in your comfy chair once everyone in your household has gone to bed or before everyone wakes up. Your surroundings are clear of distractions, so you can have time to fellowship with God. Being together but doing a lot of listening. Opening hands to how the Holy Spirit might lead in this quiet space you are lingering in. "Jesus often withdrew to lonely places and prayed" (Luke 5:16 NIV).

Healthy solitude is also more short-lived than isolation, and since we were made for being in community, it prepares us for exactly that. It's one of my favorite practices as an introvert, but it's equally important for extroverts. Solitude is life-giving, yet it's not given the proper place in our culture of striving, busyness, constant noise, and every loud intrusion that occupies our time and seems to take over our minds.

Writer Anna Rachel Bolch says, "Loneliness creates a void in our souls. Solitude fulfills us. By practicing solitude and silence, we become better observers of the noise around us. We can then discern what is from God and what is not. When we have this inner solitude, it will show itself in our outward lives."

I'm always amazed at the shift to slow living that Jesus invited others to and regularly practiced himself. He weaved solitude into his adult life on earth amid the very important work his Father had sent him here to do. Sometimes this intentional stillness looked effortless and other times deliberate. Embodiment helps us understand that Jesus was also

> *Solitude is the picnic blanket that is spread out on the landscape of our busy life.*

fully human and often experienced the real need to be immersed in quiet. That was how he was refreshed and talked to the Father.

Mark 1:35 (NIV) says, "Very early in the morning, while it was still dark, Jesus got up, left the house and went off to a solitary place, where he prayed." I love seeing an example of something simple that Jesus did. I find it fascinating that it would even be mentioned in Scripture—but since we see it in Mark, we know it is important. What if solitude is the remedy for the never-ending hustle and bustle of everyday life?

If you have trouble tuning out the noise and activity around you in a time of stillness, it can be helpful to listen to a repetitive sound like the rain falling on a tin roof or a fire crackling. You can enjoy this in real life or in podcast form. Spiritual life is not so much about *doing* as it is about *being*. If you aren't used to taking time for quiet, you may need to start with small increments of quiet music or repetitive sounds at first. If you have been on a hamster wheel, you might even fall asleep the first time you do this. That's okay. Your body may be crying out for rest.

> *What if solitude is the remedy for the never-ending hustle and bustle of everyday life?*

Arrows Pointing to Solitude

Do you find it easy or hard to make time for solitude and actively pursue it? While we need to be alone with our thoughts and have time to listen to what God is wanting to say to us, we often have to get there with the help of others. I have several "unseen mentors" in my life who pour into me from afar. I highly recommend keeping your eyes open for someone who God may be putting in your path to ever so slightly guide you in your shift to a slower pace. This person might be a spiritual director, a local friend who is a decade or two older than you, a podcaster, an author, or a grandparent.

My friend Carla H. Hayden, who is a clarity coach, has a personal practice of going on retreat by herself on a quarterly basis where she implements many slow living practices. In a conversation we had on my podcast, Carla answered two questions: What does it look like to unwind? What is the difference between relaxing and resting? She says it comes down to these four things—and she says the order is important—relax, rest, refresh, and refocus. Carla has taught me to leave the agenda up to God, thereby giving myself the space to respond to God's invitation. Carla says, "Relaxing is allowing yourself to unwind, where resting is allowing yourself to be held by God."

Like finding your island in the city, solitude is pivotal to our brains and emotions. We have to keep paying close attention to our bodies' needs, which means that we have to purposefully disconnect from things that constantly beg for our attention. You'd think our cellphones were sirens, sitting on the rocks and watching us hustle by. The lure is strong. We and our children need a rest from constant scrolling on social media and news platforms.

I used to hate having to take a nap when I was little, always afraid I would miss something. My daughter was the same way, promptly ending naps at three years old. And yet as a woman in my early fifties now, I practically adore crawling under the cold sheets for a long and fruitful rest. I try to take advantage of any chance when my body tells me she needs a nap. Albert Einstein addressed this juxtaposition when he said, "I live in that solitude which is painful in youth, but delicious in the years of maturity."

Single-tasking is the new multitasking, as we are finding out that the rewiring of our brains is also damaging to our souls. Whether you are a creative person or not, it's helpful to give yourself time and space to go inward and remove any distractions, or anything that competes with your attention. Given the common cultural message that women should be able to do many things at once, I often wonder why I can't multitask well. Most likely, I am not aware of the deep inner work going on in me, and do not realize I cannot simultaneously have deep outer things going on. Sometimes ideas in society about gender and introversion are ingrained in us despite not being a good fit.

Writer Jane Porter cites Earl Miller, a MIT neuroscientist, who says, "Our brains simply aren't built to multitask well, which means we end up diluting the quality and efficiency of what we're doing in the process." Porter goes on to say that focusing on just one thing, without allowing distractions to intrude, becomes its own form of *sacred solitude*. I, too, find that doing one thing mindfully gives me better results—not just from a productivity standpoint, but also in regulating my stress level. I like the rhythm of lower stress, and I'm sure my family and friends like that in me too.

Waiting in the Darkness

On my writing desk sits a tiny painting done by my friend Kristin Vanderlip, who writes about healing and hope. She named the painting "Dusk." The precious piece of art is a gift, a remembrance of pain we have both walked through individually. But the beauty that has struck me most lies in her own words that I asked her to pen on the back of the watercolor: "Dusk becomes a kind mercy. It is an invitation into deep rest in the waiting."

It's in the third stage of non-REM sleep that we encounter deep sleep. This is also known in scientific circles as slow-wave sleep. While you aren't aware of it, during this cycle your heartbeat slows down as does your breathing, allowing your body to fully rest. This third stage is where the slow but deep work of repair happens. And so it is with the healing journey we may find ourselves in while we cannot see the light.

Similarly, in the sacred work of soul mending, we must slow down, rest, and let the work be done in solitude, even on our behalf. This is the mercy Kristin's art piece speaks of in the resting and waiting we so often despise and question. We want fast, we want bright, we want anything other than that third stage of soul work. But we cannot bounce out of a dark night of the soul; we can only tread lightly.

Solitude is not just for our own benefit. It is fascinating how solitude actually does the legwork of preparing us for connection with others, resulting in a deeper feeling of community. When we are alone for chunks of time, we find what works for us, as opposed to getting everyone else's perspective and opinions thrown in.

My friend Honey loves to swim laps when there's a high chance of having the pool to herself. Scuba divers and snorkelers will attest to the relaxation and refreshment that come with both the sea's gentle movement and lack of noise. Being alone helps our empathy level for others rise, which begins our interactions in a more grace-filled posture. While time and perspective do their work in softening the circumstances, solitude and spaciousness do their own work in softening us.

I feel full permission to seek out solitude and silence, seeing that Jesus himself gave us a beautiful example of showing his disciples when it was time to get away. "Because so many people were coming and going that they did not even have a chance to eat, [Jesus] said to [his disciples], 'Come with me by yourselves to a quiet place and get some rest.' So they went away by themselves in a boat to a solitary place" (Mark 6:31-32 NIV).

Sounds like a really good call. If I was one of the disciples with Jesus that day, I might have gotten "hangry"—which we know can surely contribute to unkind words and behaviors toward others we are serving. Don't ask me how I know. Jesus didn't tell his disciples to run themselves ragged and not take care of their own needs. He gave a direct suggestion, and I wonder what would have happened if he hadn't.

While time and perspective do their work in softening the circumstances, solitude and spaciousness do their own work in softening us.

I trust that the verse above in Mark 6 gives you permission to find solitude and silence. This slow living shift continues to be a learning curve. Tread gently. Keep implementing solitude and silence and allow the spaciousness to settle you.

For Reflection and Discussion

How do you define solitude? Is it a scary or a comforting word for you?

Why does our society prefer information, knowledge, and noise over wonder and silence? What are some ways to shift that preference in your own life?

Can you recall a time when you knew that your soul was at rest, and it made you feel happy to be alone? What age were you?

12

A Lingering Pace with God and Others

To walk with Jesus is to walk with a slow, unhurried pace. Hurry is the death of prayer and only impedes and spoils our work. It never advances it.

JOHN MARK COMER

LINGERING WITH SOMEONE may take effort at first, but usually doesn't take effort while it's happening. The word *lingering* has a sauntering ring to it as it rolls off the tongue. A staying-just-a-little-longer feel. If you like holding a conversation with someone while you are, say, in a hot tub or walking through a rose garden, it's easy to want just five more minutes of that. I love that God is never trying to hurry us along or cuts our time short with him just when it gets good. He is the constant companion who is unchanging and has all the time in the world for us.

When I am with close friends or loved ones, I want to stretch out the time we are together and am usually in no hurry to leave. I think of the friendship that Jesus had with Mary, Martha, and Lazarus. How Jesus wept at the death of Lazarus, feeling the proximity of the "already and not yet" that we also are constantly aware of, but rarely address in our busy lives. How he spent time with them the way we spend time with our good friends—eating, laughing, and talking about life.

Lingering with God

I believe God wants that same relationship with us. It mirrors the friendship that the Trinity experienced at the beginning of time. Author Richella Parham, in her book *Mythical Me*, cites the Puritan idea that "God in himself is a sweet society." I love that we are being invited to leave room for God to show up in unique and surprising ways as we walk through our ordinary lives.

Jesus had a built-in trust and companionship with his twelve disciples, but he didn't travel the globe in his thirty-three years on earth. He spent much of it in a state of ordinary soul care, as he did his Father's work and simultaneously lived in community with his family and neighbors. We know that Jesus did a lot of walking with others, both figuratively and metaphorically. We also know that sometimes he lingered in places and took his time getting to his next destination—often at the chagrin of those waiting for him to arrive.

As I've been thinking about this intimate concept of walking with God, I ponder God walking with Adam and Eve. They literally, not metaphorically, walked in the cool of the day, lingering in the garden. Noah walked with God. His great-grandfather Enoch walked with God. I wonder what it might have looked like for my great-grandmothers to walk with God in their lifetime—both during seasons of ease and in hard times like the Great Depression.

> *Jesus did a lot of walking with others.*

Slow Living Shift
Lingering with Intention

These last few years, I've felt a big shift. It's a growing desire for a simpler, steadier existence with God, instead of a knowledge-based understanding. Ruth Haley Barton writes in her book *Sacred Rhythms*, "When we engage the Scriptures for spiritual transformation, we make it our top priority to listen to God relationally rather than seeking only to learn more about God cognitively."

We can have community with God through intentional times of stillness with God. This might look like listening for that still small voice, reading the Old and New Testaments, hearing Scripture read to us, and engaging in prayer and meditation. Each time I read the Scriptures, I see something new and marvel at how God's Word allows us to linger with him and get to know him in a fresh way on a daily basis. In addition to traditional practices, there are other ways to listen to God relationally. My friend Julianne includes activities like going for a walk, sitting on a porch, baking in the kitchen, and flower arranging. There are so many ways to linger and listen.

When we pause to think of deity arriving at humanity's doorstep in solidarity—having experienced much of what we do—the lines of this old song gloriously recorded by Merle Haggard come to life in a deeper way.

And he walks with me and he talks with me,
And he tells me I am his own.

A friend who comes to us, then gives his life for us.

Lingering allows us to hear the voice of God more distinctly. In pondering my everyday lingering with God, I find the story of God's revelation to Elijah so fascinating. I wonder if we're supposed to contemplate a bit more why God chose to come to Elijah in a gentle whisper when he passed by. Whether God was walking by or hovering near, Elijah certainly would have had to be quiet himself, slowing down to be still to wait and listen. Being completely present, attentive and full of anticipation. Lingering.

> The LORD said, "Go out and stand on the mountain in the presence of the LORD, for the LORD is about to pass by." Then a great and powerful wind tore the mountains apart and shattered the rocks before the LORD, but the LORD was not in the wind. After the wind there was an earthquake, but the LORD was not in the earthquake. After the earthquake came a fire, but the LORD was not in the fire. And after the fire came a gentle whisper. When Elijah heard it, he pulled his cloak over his face and went out and stood at the mouth of the cave. Then a voice said to him, "What are you doing here, Elijah?" (1 Kings 19:11-13 NIV)

"We may ignore, but we can nowhere evade the presence of God. The world is crowded with Him. He walks everywhere incognito." These words from C. S. Lewis really came alive for me recently when my daughter and I accompanied our friends Lissa and Emma Kate on a trip to New York City. All the people! The crowded spaces in the dim subway. The honking. The city smells. The walking we had to do to get everywhere. But in the midst of it all, whether I was distracted or not, God was walking with us—from the food truck on the corner, to the subway, the park, Soho, and Broadway. I was reminded of my island in the city metaphor, where I encourage others to pick a quiet nook in a loud and busy season of life.

One of my favorite places to silence the hustle and bustle of the honking traffic and the crowded streets was Saint Patrick's Cathedral. It was quiet, and in the hush, it became my island in the city for about twenty minutes. I slowly took in the massive space, studied the stained-glass windows, and took pictures of the ornate decor. It was beautiful. While we can find literal sanctuaries everywhere, knowing God is with us and never leaves us or forsakes us is a sacrificial kind of lingering that only he can do.

When God Sends Others to Linger with Us

There are ways to hold space for each other as we attempt to walk with others in the same quiet way that God walks with us. An aspect of walking together is just being together, even if no one speaks. It's really the opposite of hurrying.

My longtime friend Karen and I have certainly enjoyed some highs in life together. Our bucket list checkoffs include kissing the Blarney stone in Ireland, fishing and actually catching a salmon in Alaska, riding in a helicopter, and going on many beach trips. Our list also includes ordinary things like helping out in each other's wedding, dog sitting, babysitting, and meeting for the occasional coffee or lunch. But one of my favorite and most impactful memories with Karen happened when we were fairly new friends. It happened on the day that a circle of our girlfriends wanted to celebrate my thirtieth birthday at a popular restaurant.

This birthday was a first for me after becoming widowed. I wasn't prepared for the wave of sorrow that filled me that afternoon leading up to dinner. I called Karen and said I simply couldn't join in on the festivities, even though I had been looking forward to it. She offered to come over and go for a long walk with me at the lake behind my rental house instead. We were mostly quiet as we took in the beautiful scenery on the shaded paths. It became a special summer day embedded in my memory, where I saw a friend shift plans to slow down and be present, holding space for my grief. There are times when God sends someone to linger with us, a tangible demonstration of his companionship and care. These moments feel sacred if we can have eyes to see them.

> *These moments feel sacred if we can have eyes to see them.*

Lingering with Others

Culturally, this can feel a little harder to do as a society, especially here in the United States. We are generally uncomfortable with a silence which always begs to be filled with words. We long to do something tangible to make someone who is suffering feel better. Yet we are often way too busy to linger with them.

We have good intentions. Many of us want to drop off the casserole to the person who is recovering from surgery, but we don't always want to look the receiver in the eye or come inside to visit for a few minutes. I have been on both the giving and the receiving end of this. We want to say all the right things at the funeral, but sometimes a lingering smile, hug, or glance says more than words will.

Slowing down can make us feel uncomfortable, yet it is a part of building deeper relationships with those around us, through even the heaviest of seasons. Just as we can sit with God in our sorrow and lament, not saying a word, we can linger with others as we walk out swirling emotions brought on by unexpected pain and circumstances out of our control. I wonder, in earlier generations, was it always a neighborly thing to sit on the front porch together? Did communities watch out for each other, or were there years when the norm was to keep to oneself?

Author Natasha Smith discusses this idea in her book *Can You Just Sit with Me?* She has found through her own seasons of deep grief that walking with someone doesn't have to be active to be most effective. Just like we believe we are seen and held by a God named Emmanuel (which means "God with us"), we can mirror that for others by simply being with them. No agenda. No clichés. No striving to fix. Being, not doing. Just present and available. This lingering is the spiritual practice of holding space for one another. Natasha has held space for me on the phone, at a picnic table, and certainly across from each other on our many coffee dates. Her friendship has been such a gift; she is always mirroring the way God attentively lingers with us in our joys and sorrows.

As we continue to experience a chance to truly live into a slower, more meaningful way with God and with others, may we accept the Holy Spirit's gentle invitation to linger a bit longer than we have in the past.

For Reflection and Discussion

What might life have looked like for your great-grandparents? How different (or similar) did their walking with God and others look compared to yours?

What are some new ways you have sensed God walking with you lately?

Who comes to mind when you think of a friend who has sat quietly with you on a particular day or in a long, hard season?

13

Barefoot Hospitality
Means Being Present

Most humans are never fully present in the now
because unconsciously they believe that the next
moment must be more important than this one.
But then you miss your whole life,
which is never not now.

ECKHART TOLLE

I HAVE THIS DEEP NEED to have community. I also have this unfortunate trait of FOMO—the fear of missing out. When I fear missing out on some elusive next thing, I miss out on relationships and experiences standing right in front of me. Sometimes literally! When I move way too fast through life, or when I pine for more, it hurts me and it hurts others. But when I engage in an island-time way of thinking, people and things come into better focus, as they should.

What this looks like now and over the last few decades has shifted as I have changed and grown as a person. What I have learned over the years is that intentionality is everything. Slowing down to fully pay attention and notice each other is the key that unlocks this ability to be present to one another's ordinary life.

When you are comfortable and vulnerable, at home with yourself in the world, you can invite others to take their shoes off, to feel settled, grounded, and at ease. Slowing down to be hospitable to your own body and your own needs will give you the ability to show kindness and hospitality to others in your midst.

Slow Living Shift
Being Present to Others

Being present to someone takes on many shapes. Sometimes it's through action. Other times it's subtle or sacred. There is a connection that happens when we can see each other's faces that doesn't happen otherwise. Looking someone in the eyes does give a glimpse of their soul that goes deeper than making a comment on someone's social media post. Seeing my friends' faces in real time on my computer screen connects me in a way that the telephone or text just seems to miss. I recently heard about a man who visited a group home for people with visual impairments, and the first thing the children wanted to do was to feel this man's facial features up close, to "see" him with other senses, if you will.

One of my favorite jobs at age twenty-one was being a hostess at a restaurant. Our staff was trained by owners who also happened to run the second-best steakhouse in Atlanta at the time. While our restaurant was not as upscale, it did often have a two-hour wait, and we were known for our famous fried green tomatoes. However, the owners wanted the guests to feel just as special here as they did at their fancy restaurant, so we were all trained the exact same way.

I learned a lot about addressing people by their name, looking them in the eye when I spoke to them, and patiently observing where they sat in proximity to their guests or colleagues. I would mark the ticket in such a way that allowed the server to walk up,

Slowing down to fully pay attention and notice each other is the key that unlocks this ability to be present to one another's ordinary life.

pick up the ticket I had just set face down, and look directly at the "head" of the party, welcoming that person by his or her last name. It set the tone for letting them know they had chosen the right place to be nourished and taken care of—and more importantly, that they were seen as an important patron.

In biblical times, it was customary to wash feet because of dusty foot travel. In our modern world, most of us don't want someone to see our feet unless we are wearing flip-flops or are at the beach, barefoot alongside everyone else. This idea of washing another's feet represents care and service. We can incorporate this metaphor of being present to one another with what I like to call barefoot hospitality. This is a welcoming posture, where you are interested in the other person feeling safe and well taken care of in your presence.

While I have never been to a church footwashing, I recently saw a beautiful example of this in the movie *Jesus Revolution*. In the movie, a pastor's care for the hippies in his community was demonstrated through his presence as he washed the feet of everyone walking through the doors of his church. He showed them Jesus' love by replicating what Jesus did with his own disciples.

Years ago, my friend Jennie and I found a way to pay attention to others when we were trying to grow my bath and body spa line. Our mutual friends would host a handful of women in their homes for a night of relaxation and slowing down. Jennie and I would go around the room, providing a sea salt foot scrub to anyone who needed some care and refreshment. Jeans rolled up, tired feet soaking in little tubs, the women felt seen as we connected with them in this way.

Active Listening for Slow Living

Look at the amazing benefits that happen when we share what God is doing in our life with someone who wants to listen and gives us space to talk. Reverend Summer Gross says,

> When the Lord does a beautiful work within us, we have to share it with each other in order for it to crystalize even further into our neural pathways. So, that sharing isn't just a way to build community, but it's also a way of settling the truth of this work into the very foundations of our soul.

I believe that having someone hear you—truly hear you, without words and thoughts immediately being returned upon you—is one of the most beautiful experiences one can have. Most of us want to be heard without the listener giving advice, sighs, criticism, or platitudes. Whether the subject matter is big or little, having another human take in what you are saying can literally be healing.

Adam S. McHugh, author of *The Listening Life*, says:

> When we listen, we invite others into places of vulnerability and potential intimacy. If we do it right, we won't fully know

what we are getting ourselves into; we don't know who will come in and what they will bring with them. We are opening ourselves to surprise, to receiving strangers, to hearing the unexpected. We are opening ourselves to being changed.

It's what I want.

A few years ago, I was given the unbelievable pleasure of spending the weekend at a holistic soul care retreat with a group of (almost entirely) strangers. We spent chunks of time circled around the coffee table, slippers on, coffee in hand, all the while wearing our hearts on our sleeves in this cozy home setting. We found ourselves in a safe space surrounded by safe people. Bekah Pogue, our host and facilitator who is also a certified spiritual director, is someone I like to think of as a gracious soul-carer.

I did not realize at first that walking through precious pockets of time—where time itself stood still—would heal the soul. But I quickly learned. The magic that happened among us at our long-awaited Pasture Experience Retreat was not necessarily because wisdom was given, deep words were spoken, or even solid answers were dancing in front of us.

It was in the silence that the beauty unfolded for each one of us. Time and space seemed to pause as we took long turns listening to each person, with not so much as a raised hand, a head nod, an amen, or a good word. I'm not saying those actions are wrong, but in the setting of co-listening or coming alongside one another, silence was our golden key there. Some words were uttered out loud by participants for the first time ever.

To be able to whisper long-caged-up words and articulate thoughts that might have never been spoken out loud before while looking into the faces of women who were strangers just the day before was beyond incredible. Each person knew that boldness, risk, vulnerability, and trust were swirling in the room all around us and between us. There was unseen, but somehow tangible, grace.

This experience was new for me. To be in a place of unraveling, of pondering, of knowing, of "me too," but nodding in agreement with our eyes and not our voice or body was invaluable. To have the floor, so to speak, when it was your turn.

It's a natural tendency for us to want to rescue others with our ideas and words. We are a society that likes to give advice and we think we are always right. Or at least I often do. It takes a shifting to relax, to be unhurried, and give someone's chance of private restoration a shot. There is solidarity in the stillness. The very act of being present while quiet together is powerful. There is a freedom in expressing your deepest wounds and joys without feeling the need to be defensive. A figurative table where you have a seat with your name on it, just because you are a person made in God's image. With no need to explain yourself to anyone, you find that you are seen and heard. And that is enough.

These little flashes of delight, of co-listening, can also be experienced with just one or two friends, right in your hometown. It might be during early spring while sitting in lawn chairs under an old oak tree. It can be experienced on a girls' weekend while walking on the beach together—making footprints in the sand and letting words get caught up in the wind and blown out to sea. Or maybe it'll be during winter, while you are curled up on a couch, cradling a cup of hot tea. Let each other's words flow until there are no more. Pauses and spaces of silence are gifts, not reasons to feel uncomfortable. This attunement is important. Sometimes the body needs an extra moment to catch up with a thought, feeling, or word.

Active listening in this busy world is even possible in the back rooms of social media, on text, or on the walkie-talkie app Voxer. Simply acknowledging a friend with a DM saying, "I hear you," or a voice message saying, "I see you," may be enough. I know, because I've experienced these moments in real life. I have been both the quiet listener as well as the one exposing my heart with many jumbled words.

These sacred experiences are what I call community for your soul.

If at times, we become silent before our Creator to hear him well, doesn't it also make sense to be still with others to hear them too? We hear a lot about grace—in devotionals, on Instagram, in the church. But grace and space truly are what we need to put another person's needs front and center to offer attunement. It's the slowing down that brings life. Sometimes talking out loud is all that is needed to feel validated. Sometimes the quiet that follows someone's words is the gift.

It Is a Choice to Embrace Another's Experience

Awareness is always a good thing. We have the choice to embrace another's experience instead of dismissing it or competing with it. Our stories matter. They shape who we have been and who we have become. To listen to and honor each other's experience is a huge part of slowing down and truly seeing another human being made in the image of God. We will have a difficult time understanding someone's life if we only skim their headlines and never look into the whole story of what makes them shine in the world as their true self. Likewise, our hearts will have a hard time softening to the plight of others if we do not take the time to hear someone's backstory, family history, or season of suffering.

You don't have to know my whole story to have compassion for me. And likewise, I don't have to even agree with the way you see the world to show you kindness and solidarity. Slowing down to hear each other's stories becomes a pivotal connection point whether in the online world or right in our neighborhoods and local communities.

Our stories matter. They shape who we were and who we have become.

We do not always get to choose how we are perceived, received, or treated. We are taught to give one another the benefit of the doubt, but without slowing down to fully see where someone is coming from, we will often be misunderstood or dismissed. It is one reason I am so passionate about more slow and intentional living, especially if you are a Christ-follower. As people, we all want to feel secure and to be seen. Those are words that simply indicate a compassionate noticing.

While we will never experience the depth of someone else's life circumstances, I have seen over and over the times when God lets you have a tiny glimpse into another's life. Sometimes this happens as you are a bystander, and other times it happens when you yourself go through an experience that makes you pause and hold space for another's situation. This is simply awareness. It's slowing down just enough to be open minded and see the bigger picture of how life is playing out.

When this happens, the impact is life-changing, and gives you a deeper perspective that you wouldn't have even considered. It's like standing at one of those large coin-operated binocular viewing machines where you put in a quarter and put your eyes up to the lens. As the place you are looking toward comes into clearer focus, you see a distinct picture of something you've never noticed or don't usually have the opportunity to see.

One of my favorite connections that came from slowing down happened on a retreat years ago. Up on a balcony, a group of us were sitting in rocking chairs overlooking a lake, and we could see steps descending in the distance out of the side of the cliff below. Karin, who sat next to me, smiled as she glanced into the distance. At the very same time, we both mouthed the words, "Reminds me of 1000 Steps." Shocked, we looked at each other quizzingly, not sure we had heard the other correctly. I laughed awkwardly and said that my "1000 Steps" was on a remote island in the Caribbean, my childhood home. Karin's eyes grew wide as she nodded and said, "Mine too. Bonaire?"

Turns out, Karin and her husband, Ed, had some of their favorite vacations while scuba diving at the various reefs around Bonaire, and she was very familiar with the location that held a special place in my heart. I cannot imagine missing this profound moment in time! I am so glad that in my moment of wondering if I even belonged in this group of people, God opened up a memory and a pocket of vulnerability where Karin and I both shared something out loud that spoke volumes of solidarity to my heart and hers. Sometimes our stories intersect in the most beautiful and fantastic ways!

Noticing the Painful and Hard Things

What is our vantage point in observing something? How do we see it from where we are standing now and the limited knowledge we might have? When we are aware of our surroundings and the people moving through our midst, we offer our time and attention as a gift. Slow living causes us to notice painful and hard things.

Some things need to stay in the light to help us slow down enough to really pay attention to those details illuminating the past. Through the generations, pieces of history beg for a truer story to be told through word of mouth, so that we continue the slow steady work of loving God and loving others. Honoring those who have gone before us comes from the work of slowing down to notice.

> *Slow living causes us to notice painful and hard things.*

Out on the south side of Bonaire, there is a row of small white huts made of stone and facing the gorgeous sea. When I made plans to take my husband Dean to visit Bonaire, I knew that I wanted to spend some time out at this historic landmark. It's not too far from the salt flats and the radio towers that my dad's friend Denny used to climb.

As a child, I would often linger in these various huts, feeling the cool floor, running my hands along the walls, wondering what it would be like to live in these, not being fully aware of the dark history and painful stories they held.

These little dwellings were built in the 1850s as sleeping quarters that held six male slaves per hut. These men mined the salt flats, laboring in the hot sun and strong trade winds. When I was a little girl, I could walk straight into these tiny huts. But as the years went by and I grew taller, I had to crouch down to go in or out of them.

The Bonaire salt mines and the slave trade were at the center of trade for over two centuries between West Africa, Spain, and the thirteen US colonies. Salt was as valuable as silver and gold.

Returning to the location as an adult, I found myself sitting in the same place I did as a child—the openings that faced the sparkling blue Caribbean Sea in those huts. But I was aware that much heavier stories lay behind my childhood memories. In this very place lay the heavy stories of the men who crouched to enter and exit from that same seaside two centuries before me.

While we cannot undo the past, we can slow down to learn about and honor the people who were present at that time. Sometimes that means leaving history in plain view where the full story can be a solemn symbol of remembrance for generations to come. A small glimpse doesn't give you a full knowledge of something, but it can awaken awareness that creates curiosity and clarity. It allows us to better attune to the needs of each other, where we can validate and affirm one another. This is an active part of loving God and loving others that we read about in the New Testament. In a world that is not usually others-focused, it takes work to notice—to slow down our busy lives and show compassion.

For Reflection and Discussion

How easy or hard is it for you to stay present with someone?

Have you experienced a scenario where people felt safe to talk and the ones listening let the one talking completely "have the floor," so to speak? How could you benefit from someone just listening and not giving advice?

Have you noticed painful or hard things when you've stepped back to observe something or someone? What have you noticed?

PART TWO

BENEDICTION

In this season of weariness
and unending obligations,
May you embrace the
importance of trading
busyness for listening.
As you shift your focus from
striving to lingering—in
solitude and prayer—
May your overwhelm be
replaced by your desire to
be fully present with Jesus.

PART THREE

You Are Free to Live Slow

The things that matter most
should never be at the mercy of
the things that matter least.

JOHANN WOLFGANG VON GOETHE

14

You've Had Permission All Along

She silently stepped out of the race she never wanted to be in, found her own lane, and proceeded to win.

PAM LAMBERT

THERE IS FREEDOM IN UNDERSTANDING that we can name our pace. While the journey of shifting into a different gear is never quite linear, thankfully, the answers we crave can often be simple and straightforward. I continuously reread this thought by Pam Lambert, which so beautifully captures exactly what I want for women and men who long for that exhale, that slower pace. Finding my own lane, and then having the liberty to stay there, keeps me focused on my own calling in life. I hope it gives you as much freedom as it has me. I don't know Pam personally, but if this quote isn't Pam throwing us a lifeline, I don't know what is. Grab on to it, friend.

This shift is about slower living, but at the same time, it's about so much more. It's not even about winning. It's about inhaling fresh beauty, seeing and understanding your reality, building deeper community, and, ultimately, trusting God.

Slow Living Shift
Being Empowered

Who and what has been keeping you from slowing down? No one can dictate your life's pace to you. It is your divine right to inhale and exhale—not just in the literal sense, but in ways that are life-giving and sustainable.

It's courageous to stand up for your needs. You don't have to be exhausted all of the time; our bodies and minds need an exhale. Brené Brown says, "If we want to live a wholehearted life, we have to become intentional about cultivating sleep and play, and about letting go of exhaustion as a status symbol and productivity as self-worth."

Perhaps you wonder if you'll be missing out on something, or if you are letting others down with your decision. I still do sometimes. But only you know the things that matter most to you. Own the idea that you're in charge of your life's rhythms and commitments. The busyness, the hustle, and the opinions of others aren't.

There are three questions that are important to ask yourself when you feel the urge to slow down, but those old feelings start creeping back in. So stop and ask:

Is this true?

Examples of lies we believe:

- I am the only one who can get this done or everything will crumble.
- If I don't participate, I'll lose favor with this group or particular person and will let them down.

- This will put me back a little bit in my own goals, energy, or money, but I'm pretty sure I can make up for the lost time and sleep somehow.

Is this even reasonable?

Examples of unreasonable burdens:

- Adding this extra errand for a family member into my day, or doing a two-hour favor for someone at school on my weekend off, will derail time promised to my child or partner.
- It will keep me from settling down my own nervous system with something relaxing.
- It will use up my own energy reserves after my recent illness.

What am I leaving in the wake of this decision?

Examples of consequences:

- It will cause me to let down the people I have already committed to, which is not fair to them and is detrimental to the trust we've established.
- Since I didn't have time to cook at home, I'm now spending money on getting last-minute takeout using money meant for something else I had planned on this week, which is a disappointment.
- My body will most likely require an extra day for recovery, so I'll be putting off what I had planned for tomorrow; it was really important to me.

Is More Really Merrier? Choose Wisely

You are empowered to decide who is in your inner circle and when. We are not only influenced by our culture but by people who do not have the same ideals as we do. If you are not aligned with someone who is trying to speak into your life, then you have the freedom to set gentle boundaries in place.

Who came up with the phrase "the more the merrier" anyway? I often cringe whenever I hear someone utter these words. Not because I am antisocial, but because I know that for every "win" in adding one more person to the scene, there is often an unseen "loss" involved. The result is counter to what we may think; hang with me for a bit, as I trust you'll find some much-needed freedom from obligations here. Let's look at the benefits of a smaller circle, in which we ask God if we are to be present with a few instead of with many.

Who came up with the phrase "the more the merrier" anyway?

Author and speaker Dharius Daniels says in his book *Relational Intelligence*, "Relational intelligence is the ability to discern if someone should be a part of our lives and what place they should occupy, and then align them accordingly." I think this idea is brilliant, and it solves a lot of hospitality dilemmas. But we must slow down if we are to practice it.

Think of your own ideal family dinnertime. It's summertime and everyone is home. You were hoping to have a safe space for your children to talk about their day and get their veggies in, and for you and your spouse to decompress over some comfort food, but now two neighborhood kids knock on the door to play. Of course, they haven't eaten dinner, because the moon is not out yet. Your teens pipe up, "Hey, can they eat with us too?" And your spouse turns and says, "Of course. The more the merrier."

This dilemma is all about expectation and communication. It might be a good time to ponder the question we asked earlier: Is this even reasonable?

As the noise level and laughter escalates with two additional people at the table, the family meal is gobbled up quickly and the dirty dishes start clanking. The noise is not just swirling in the room, it's also churning in your mind. If something feels chaotic or intrusive, it's not unkind to set up gentle boundaries. This is part of slower living.

You have to decide whether the unexpected way dinner just played out was a fun memory in the making. Was there much-needed laughter, generosity, spontaneity, and something you'll talk about years from now? Or did this take an already tense family situation and throw an opportunity out the window? Did you miss the opportunity to connect with one of your teenagers' life challenges? Did this act of hospitality throw the normal and healthy rhythm of the household into chaos for the rest of the evening? Maybe the one person who needed the safety and proximity of the family dinner ended up feeling invisible and unheard.

As a former missionary kid, I have heard lamentable stories of children and teenagers—who are now adults—feeling like they were chosen last or glossed over for important ministry and visitors. Often, when our family was on furlough in the United States, my dad would head out to give a talk, usually at a Sunday night church service where my parents were raising support. Seeing that we were tired and "peopled out" already, my mom would stay home with us; we'd enjoy supper followed by a quiet evening, allowing us to regroup and get some sleep.

In the last few years, I've often thanked my parents for their care and flexibility during my childhood. I have come to realize that their slowing down and choosing time with me during these busy seasons of ministry wouldn't always have been a popular choice for them to make and I don't want to take any sacrifice for granted. But what they modeled was that making their kids a priority was a ministry in and of itself, keeping a secure attachment a priority in their calling and kingdom work. Especially for me—this introverted, highly sensitive daughter.

Kindness in community may mean being inclusive. But kindness also means being wise and valuing individuals as much as the whole. Sometimes unexpected visitors do funnel charity, belonging, and kindness into one big offering of our time and resources. But we can also guard our energy and capacity by learning from these impromptu happenings and set a foundation for what would be best for everyone going forward. You can learn when it is totally appropriate to open your door to others while also seeking the freedom to tell others that now is not a good time.

> *Kindness in community may mean being inclusive. But kindness also means being wise and valuing individuals as much as the whole.*

From personal experience, I can tell you that while there's never a perfect answer, more often than not, trying to be overly inclusive has made everyone more stressed. I have needed a listening ear, but instead was lost in the crowd. I have noticed a weary look and wanted to help, but instead got caught up in being everyone's friend in the moment.

For cocktails and a movie, more may, in fact, be merrier. In such a context, people will mingle and find one-on-one time with several people. But when we desire an intimate conversation that could bring life to someone who has no other social place to chat, or simply because we have been walking life together for several years, the letdown of not being seen or heard can hamper the relationship. We might miss deep conversations; perhaps, on one long-awaited girls' night, the crucial story of a wayward child never surfaces because several more women have joined at the last minute. If this is your story, you know that the cost is too high. Of course, at other times, we do ourselves and everyone a favor by including others on the fly. Trust your gut as you set gracious boundaries.

Ask yourself:

- *why* you are changing plans at the last minute
- *who* you might be trying to please
- *how* that will impact the trust of the people who have already set aside this time to intentionally gather with you
- *where* you will now congregate, and if there is enough room to add people
- *when* you can spend some personal time soon with the person you originally made plans with, if your group dynamics change and expand

Being others-focused also means knowing our people well, which cannot happen if we spread ourselves too thin. If I have already planned an intimate dinner with two people whose love language is quality time, yet invite additional friends at the last minute, I just did a disservice to the relationship I have been building with those two friends.

But if you or I have just been introduced to a new person, say, in the church foyer or on the school grounds, who has recently moved to town and is putting themselves out there to find a safe community, it's reasonable and kind to invite them along to get ice cream or walk around the county fair with our group of friends.

I'm sure you've heard the idea that every time you say yes to one thing, you are saying no to something else. Likewise, every time I say yes to someone, I am saying no to someone else—a real person with real feelings and expectations who I may have already committed to. Only I myself can know if my motivations are coming from that people-pleasing place, or if I am hearing someone else in my ear and not my own voice. I've learned to pause to consider the situation and everyone's expectations before blurting out those famous words, "Of course, join us. The more the merrier." This pays dividends for relationship-building in the long run.

Permission to Go Deep Instead of Wide

Something I didn't know I needed so badly was the delight of being part of a soul care mastermind group. This is a group of six women who are in the same vocation. We are a mix of writers, podcasters, artists, speakers, spiritual directors, and contemplatives.

Although our ages are different and we all live in different states, we have a lot in common: the foundation of our writing life is built upon deep soul care. Not only do we make it a priority to find both large and small pockets of time for solitude, creativity, spiritual formation practices, and writing, but we also gather on Zoom or occasionally in person to check in on each other, support one another through the everydayness of our writing lives, and ask about the joys and sorrows of each season. We hold space for one another as we walk alongside each soul sister in her celebrations and in her lament.

This small circle of women gives me the courage to keep going when the work is lonely and deadlines are looming. We have walked each other through family issues, surgeries, car accidents, overseas travel adventures, book contracts, parenting dilemmas, the loss of loved ones, and even the birth of a new baby. We don't actually talk much about the ever-changing algorithms on social media or tiny details of grammar. While that is not off the table, the focus remains on doing the hard, long, sacred work of crafting our words, first for ourselves and then for our readers.

Some of this can only be done well in a small circle. It would not be merrier, reasonable, or beneficial to add more people to our group. The vulnerability and trust we have built is precious to us. While we do not hoard this trust, we do savor and protect it so that we can be the best versions of ourselves, without falling into the trap of being all things to all people.

There are always consequences to deciding things too fast, so it's reasonable to take a moment to choose what's best for everyone in each situation. Jesus fed the five thousand on a hillside. I can just imagine all of the eager faces and hungry bellies a few hours into this gathering. He cared deeply for them. However, Jesus did not include them at the Last Supper—or every time he visited at Mary, Martha, and Lazarus's house. Again, he cared deeply, but also knew so much about really seeing people. Being hospitable has many sides to it.

For Reflection and Discussion

How do you feel knowing that you've always had permission to slow down?

What does the phrase "the more the merrier" conjure up in you when you hear it? What else can you add to the decision-making process besides asking the *why, who,* and *how* of adding people at the last minute?

How will you carry through the slow living practice of being present?

15

Burnout Behind Church Doors

Your personhood is far more important than
your productivity. You are beautiful because
the fingerprints of God mark you. Your goodness
has everything to do with your humanity and
nothing to do with your ability to fall in line.

Jenai Auman

I WOULD BE REMISS to write this book full of life-giving, slow living, and soul care advice without also mentioning one of the biggest (and unspoken) reasons that women of faith and their families are experiencing burnout today. No matter how carefully you practice soul care, if you're allowing spiritual institutions to dictate your pace, you'll never be able to take complete ownership of it.

Pushback at Church

Sometimes it's in the most unexpected places where pushback occurs. Places where we thought we could make a difference. Places where we longed for connection and community, where we sought safety in our faith journey. The joy of volunteerism can sour quickly when we experience the effects of hustle within a faith setting such as a church, life group, or Bible study. Such places may resemble a religious or spiritual experience that was life-changing for us in the past, like a week of VBS, youth group, or summer camp.

The joy of volunteerism can sour quickly when we experience the effects of hustle.

Burnout can happen for many reasons, but in church settings, it's easy for people pleasing, faith, guilt, and kingdom work to get mixed together; the waters of volunteerism and vocation start to get muddy. Being worn out causes people of faith to sometimes become disillusioned in their walk with God and others. It takes an emotional toll, and motivation usually goes right out the window along with positive attitudes and open and willing hands. It's often difficult for someone to give words to their stress and emotional exhaustion, so the burnout is interpreted as ineffectiveness, lack of interest, or not being a team player. They may feel unappreciated, unseen, and unheard.

Burnout occurs often when expectations are too high for the average person. Everyone's capacity is different; even highly energetic people have seasons where they are being pulled in many directions and simply can't keep up. When a person does too much of one thing while not getting emotional and physical support, without the chance for a break or a graceful phase-out of the work, the body and the mind start stepping up to get attention by shutting down.

In order to make the most of pausing and slowing down to find your soul's pace, you have to believe that it applies to all areas of your life, including your church life.

Many religious circles and churches push congregants to give of themselves, no matter how tiring it is, because it's kingdom work. I've watched too many people run around ragged, holding to the idea that it's "just what we do," or, "If I don't do it, no one will." While this is certainly not true of every church, can we pause here for a moment and ask: Does it have to be this way? Is it even reasonable? For church leaders or for the congregations? Many religious institutions and ministries will naturally say an enthusiastic yes to having more volunteers helping. But rest assured, human value is not determined by offering help, donating money, or sacrificing time.

Slow Living Shift
Boundaries in Faith Settings

This might be the hardest chapter for yours truly, an Enneagram Nine who despises conflict, to write. I also know it could end up being the most impactful chapter, so I will tread gently, while at the same time advocating strongly for all the women who love Jesus and crave a place of belonging in the local church today.

It took my own doctor insisting I lower my stress for me to make my own important shift. She surprised me by pushing for me to start saying no to my various activities in ministry and church volunteering when my daughter was elementary age. I had a long season where I forgot how to say no. I wanted to be involved in super exciting and, in my judgment, "worthy" opportunities to give my precious time at church.

I simply can't take on as much as other people around me; I experienced, once again, what happens when slowing down is chosen for us. That Halloween, I recall sitting on a beach chair in my driveway, wrapped in a blanket, unable to walk around the neighborhood with my husband and young daughter. I was recovering from a bout of pneumonia, Strep, and bronchitis that hit like a hurricane. It wasn't the first time this had happened, and it wouldn't be the last. I finally learned to listen to my body as it was trying to give me signals as to what my true pace should be for optimal health.

So, if this is you, I want you to know that I see your weariness amid the platitudes and loud voices asking for more volunteers for the kingdom of God. I know what various forms of burnout look like. Whether you are a church employee, a longtime member, or a new eager visitor, I want to give you the freedom to voice out loud: "No, I cannot help out at the last minute. Yes, I still love God, the church, and her people." I pray this chapter becomes your permission slip, in case you're in danger of repeating some of my people-pleasing mistakes.

Most of us are not superwomen and cannot be stretched beyond our capacity without hurting those closest to us. We can love God and love people in so many different ways: behind church doors, out at the grocery store, or in our own homes. But when our own health starts to suffer, our children miss Mom, and our life partner wonders why we have another committee meeting—a pause and reflection becomes not just a good idea, but the very thing that will keep our marriages stronger, our parent-child relationships precious, and our blood pressure lower.

There is no highest calling in slower living. Only calling. Only what God has already prepared in advance for you to do. Nothing can happen outside of God's plan, because we're part of his plan.

We're part of his story. But sometimes in our people pleasing, we may elevate our church involvement or volunteering over other people and life obligations.

What if God is not actually asking us to rate our church volunteering higher than our secular job, our time with our children, our neighbors, our aging parents, or our mental health? We deceive ourselves when we believe we are needed at the detriment of our health, our time, our energy, and our family relationships.

It feels good to be needed. It feels even better to not spread yourself so thin.

While I don't feel guilty about it, I regret a season of being overly involved in church activities when I lived in Georgia. I distinctly recall walking in the door late one evening, after a week of being out almost every night for a banquet, a missions meeting, a Bible study, and something else. Brian was watching television by himself and turned to say hello. He simply asked if I was going to be doing church stuff all the time: he missed me. We weren't doing life together; I was busy and starting to get worn out, doing important things for the kingdom, but neglecting one of the most treasured relationships God had given me at the time.

It feels good to be needed. It feels even better to not spread yourself so thin.

Brian's life-altering accident happened only a few short weeks after that, but the wake-up call was too late. We would never again have the life we once had; I could never take back the time I had already given to what I had wrongly thought was my highest calling. Thankfully, I was given a second chance to do things differently in my second marriage. These healthier boundaries outside of my home have given Dean, Lili, and me more peace and time together inside of our home.

It's okay to use firm but gentle brushstrokes when saying no to the person who gives you a hard time for painting boundaries around yourself. They simply may not understand the energy you do not have, the time you cannot afford to lose, or the passions and projects already taking up sacred space in your life's color palette.

> *It's okay to use firm but gentle brushstrokes when saying no to the person who gives you a hard time for painting boundaries around yourself.*

Life is hard enough as it is. We don't need to add to our plates in ways that result in possible bitterness, resentment, or burnout, especially in faith communities. This often leads to a skewed way of seeing our Good Shepherd. Hearing his still, small voice will often guide us through the right decision when we start feeling guilty for pausing and saying no. Burnout from trying to do more than we have capacity for is part of the price we pay for believing the lie that we need to do it all to be strong, competent humans in God's upside-down kingdom.

Could it be that the greatest work ever done was when Christ went to the cross for humankind? That after that work, no particular callings are more significant than others? What if we saw each other's giftedness, whether in music, preaching, building maintenance, or secretarial skills, as being on equal ground? Our feet would not slip as easily, because we would be rooted in community and all be on level ground inside and outside of the church doors.

Paul writes: "As it is, there are many parts, but one body. The eye cannot say to the hand, 'I don't need you!' And the head cannot say to the feet, 'I don't need you!' . . . so that there should be no division in the body, but that its parts should have equal concern for each other" (1 Corinthians 12:20-21, 25 NIV).

It seems almost ridiculous to say that an eye or a hand can do everything we need done. But if we stop and think about how the body of Christ consists of many parts, and Paul says the parts of the body (the church) should have equal concern for each other, let's take that at face value. Burnout causes high turnover in both paid church leadership and in volunteer positions. People are not machines, and the church is not a factory. If one person is doing too much and there are no able bodies to come aboard, then maybe aspects of the program or the activity that is lacking volunteers need to be adjusted and expectations lowered.

Throw Me a Life Preserver, Please

Needing each other within a faith community can and should go both ways. Leaders in the church—even paid ones—should not carry the brunt of the work and exhaust themselves, their staff, and church members. At the same time, volunteers should also not work themselves to death in picking up the pieces so things appear to run smoothly or so that they find favor or eliminate their guilt. Like a car with a broken fuel gauge running out of gas, the problem won't be evident until it is too late, until the car must slowly pull over to the side of the road and announce to passersby that it's plumb out of gas—it's "done." But it will announce it loud and clear despite the driver needing to get to a meeting or a wedding. There's just simply nothing left in the tank.

I distinctly recall a time when my husband Dean and I knew we needed to walk away from a church situation. On more than one occasion, we have realized after it's too late that we overstayed. While we respected the leadership and were friends with many people there, the pastoral hope was that we would link arms and make a fresh way for growth and sustainability. What some people didn't understand was that we were not only burned out in many different ways, we felt like we were in a fast-moving stream and had to pull ourselves onto the embankment to catch our breath. We were in the Abyss and needed to rest on the soft white sand for a while.

When someone is thrown a life preserver, they generally don't float for a minute and then take it off; they would drown. They keep the lifesaving ring on until they have reached safety, usually with another person close by, then they rest until they can get back on their feet again. And when they get up, they don't go right back out into the currents that almost took them under; they tend to other things that their body and mind need. This might look like fresh water, some protein and carbs, a soft, dry towel, maybe a Tylenol, maybe even a good cry, some deep breathing, and sleep. And that is putting it mildly.

You may have fallen into the familiar trap of being needed over your actual capacity and personhood. Currently, your giftings may be overlooked in lieu of a yes-man or someone who appears to be shinier. And if you are a pastor, or married to one, I am so sorry if you have been denied the gift of a much-needed sabbatical.

What if we could slow down to see one another's signs of distress before it's too late? My hope is that we can put forth the effort to "read the room" in the house of God.

Oh, that we would come alongside each other and check in more frequently to see the status of each other's bandwidth and spirit. The risk, of course, is that another person will either feel weak for speaking up about their need to dial back, or that they will actually be honest and we will need to find a new volunteer sooner than anticipated—or, worse yet, pick up the slack ourselves.

But what if it isn't really slack? *What if it's excess?* Like the extra green bean casserole and Jell-O brought to the potluck! Likely, no one will complain if it's not there. More often than not, no one will even notice. Perfection need never trump kindness, whether in music performance, teaching, or taking out the trash. Simple can not only be good, but be healthy in the life of a congregation, whether that church holds a hundred people or a few thousand precious souls.

> *What if we could slow down to see one another's signs of distress before it's too late? My hope is that we can put forth the effort to "read the room" in the house of God.*

A Secret Phrase to Help You Say No . . .

As I've learned to say no, I've found myself struggling with setting boundaries: "How do I say no to my church leadership? Won't I be letting someone down? My gut tells me to speak up, but my introverted side is peeking out. They say they need me, and I don't want to disappoint someone, but I know I need to decline their request."

Here's my secret phrase I pull out when I need to say no:

I very genuinely say, *"I'm going to have to pass. Thank you."*

It seems so simple, but it tells your hearers the solid action you'll take. You aren't obligated to tell the person why you cannot say yes at this time, only that you will need to pass this opportunity by. Your brain may tell you it's no big deal to speak up, but your body will tell a different story. Listen. Be gentle. This is gracious boundary setting. This is ordinary empowerment and a part of communicating in life so that others don't sabotage your serious attempts to live slowly.

There are times when our "no, thank you" needs to become permanent. Sometimes we don't know if leaving is the right thing to do. If you have needed to shift—to step away from your church, your small group, your Bible study, your place of employment, your faith-based community—you may be feeling a mixture of feelings. You may notice relief, fear, anger, grief, heartache, or a void. I pray that you will be afforded a few conversations with safe friends who gently hold your heart and your concerns with you. Ask God to help you be wise and yet unoffendable. After much solitude, contemplation, and seeking God, I pray you will know you made the best decision at the time.

While many people get shamed for "throwing in the towel" too early, others are harmed by staying longer than is necessary for their emotional and spiritual health. I'm not going to give you a platitude here, but I will say that over the years, God has always made a way when things looked bleak. Even lately, he has given me the fortitude to persevere when I need to. But he has given me the courage to step down and out as well. I know he will do the same for you if that is where you find yourself today.

For Reflection and Discussion

Has there been a time when you should have said no to helping out at church? Did you need a life preserver, or you did say no before you burned out?

How easy or hard will it be to use gracious boundaries? When will the pain of your situation be greater than your fear of standing up for yourself?

How important is rest in the ministry or church you work or volunteer in?

16

Soft White Sand Beyond the Abyss

When you go through deep waters,
I will be with you.
When you go through rivers of difficulty,
you will not drown.

Isaiah 43:2 NLT

By now, it would be of no surprise to you that most of my swim lessons as a child were in the turquoise sea. Our time was overseen by Mr. Eddy, a strong, kind man native to the island of Bonaire. Most lessons started with us all jumping off a large concrete pier into the crystal-clear waters below. Large pieces of broken, fine china plates fell downward through the sea toward the sand. They were ours to retrieve, like a treasure. Bonaire is known for crystal-clear waters; you can see down sixty feet with just a mask and snorkel. We simply opened our eyes in the saltwater and let the sunrays guide us down to the shattered, patterned flatware resting on the seabed.

During these weekly lessons, we would also relay from the pier out to the large sailboats anchored past the dark blue line, known to young minds as the Abyss. I don't know if I was the only girl who felt this way, but these unknown dark waters always frightened me into swimming like I was an Olympic athlete in the race of her life on live television. The drop-off was visibly terrifying and we knew from scuba pictures—or just walking past the open fish market—what lived down there in the deep blue sea. My mantra during these relays was: *Hold your breath. Close your eyes. Swim fast.* I certainly wish I had known about the spiritual practice of breath prayers back then, but who knows? Maybe I did modified prayers. I bet you probably have too.

We would swim as fast as our light and dark arms and legs could take us, flying through the sparkling sea, around the back end of those seaworthy boats and back into the perceived safety of the turquoise waters. All the while we trusted that Mr. Eddy, our shepherd of the sea, who made us swim in the West Indies salt water, would never take his eyes from us during our short voyages under the noonday sun. As I approached the target, fear and exhilaration splashed around in a dance. The shadows of the bow on the water, mixed with the urgency of just having crossed over that distinct line where the aquamarine shimmer hits the blue-black deepness, would have provided the perfect time to quietly recite the comforting words of Psalm 23.

While I cannot recall exactly what I prayed or pondered, I do remember many a Saturday morning going over to an elderly church member's house to recite my weekly Scripture memory verse. It's amazing what comes to mind during our younger years of spiritual formation! Young imaginations are always alive and healthy, and no doubt on swim days I was living in my very own psalm.

Right through the valley of the shadow of death.

Where I will fear no evil green moray eel or nurse shark.

I will swim over a table made of delicate coral fans in the presence of my enemies—those rarely-seen, long-winged stingrays and often-stepped-on black sea urchins.

Surely, silver barracudas and colorful parrotfish shall follow me all the days of my life. O Lord, may I dwell back on the soft white sand forever. Amen.

And then, before I knew it, I was headed back to safety, where my friends were also getting out of the water. Nearby, the stretch of soft, white sand offered a warm resting place to catch our breath. I was quite used to the sea. The salty taste of it had been on my lips since infancy. Nonetheless, the delicate, warm, grainy sand on the beach that often clung to me like a web gave me comfort. If you've ever fallen asleep on the warm sand, you know it's really hard to want to get back up.

The Shepherd of the Sea Is Near

If you are immersed in the dark Abyss today, do you see your stretch of soft white sand in the distance? Perhaps it beckons you to comfort and safety, like the light from a lighthouse. It might be knowing there is a safe friend you can call who will hear your lament. It might be taking a mental health day to get some extra sleep, or simply enjoying fresh air right in your own backyard.

Inevitably we might be pondering if we have to go to swim practice again next week. Or next year. Or again when we're older. But the Shepherd of the Sea will lead us to still waters, to green pastures, to our stretch of soft white sand just beyond the Abyss. Almighty Creator, I am expectant. I am holding open hands. My hope is in you.

Slow Living Shift

Expectancy

Often in life we can observe both fear of the unknown and a firm foundation holding hands. Just as Mr. Eddy kept his gaze on all our movements, we can rest assured that God is watching us swim near the Abyss in our most difficult seasons. But we can also breathe easier knowing there will surely be pockets of time where the soft, white, sandy beach, just beyond the dark Abyss, is our sanctuary. We can safely smile, and we can cry, maybe all in the same few minutes.

As a naive but happy elementary-aged child, I hadn't yet experienced other island adventures that would mark my years in the seventies and eighties, like that whale shark who was easily twice the size of our sailboat. That felt over-the-top for two teenagers, my friend Geoff and I, taking a fifteen-foot Sunfish out by ourselves and doing a jibe in the dark part of the sea. Then there was the time my friend Michelle, with her eyes round like saucers, pointed out the slender but predatory barracuda chasing us. And I cannot forget the annoyed squid who shot out purple ink at our family on our moonlit shore walk, all because we got too close. Not to mention the gentle but massive eagle ray who circled my pregnant mother when she was standing in the water one afternoon!

The Shepherd of the Sea will lead us to still waters.

Thankfully, I didn't know how many of these adventures would occur, or I would have tried to swim on top of the water in those swim lessons.

Little did I know that while the little blonde girl in the turquoise sea would endure adventures much harder than swimming in the blue-black Abyss, she would also be held tight and eventually learn to trust in her Shepherd of the Sea.

Despite my fears, my excitement, and everything in between, I had to trust Mr. Eddy as he stood and watched us, believing that he wouldn't put our lives at risk under the hot sun and that we would somehow return from each lap in one piece. Some days I wished that he was in the water with us. But most of the time, I preferred to look up at any wild, random moment, squinting in the sun. I always expected to see his silhouette, like a statue, guarding our lives. And he did not disappoint.

Are you in a place right now where all you can do is close your eyes, swim as hard and fast as you can, trusting God till you leave the black water and get back in the turquoise waters? I see you. I know what it's like to swallow too much saltwater and to feel like your muscles are burning because you are flying through the sea. Not just as a kid, but as a college student, a new wife, a tired mom, a disappointed friend, and a late employee. God sees you too, my friend. He is with you and knows exactly where you are, because he's never taken his eyes off you.

When we are scared, when we are approaching the Abyss or submerged in it, it's likely that we feel like Jonah. I recently reread this whale of a tale in the Old Testament, and it's amazing how we as human beings in this modern age will be able to resonate with Jonah in this unique story. My pastor, Kenny, gave words to how we might be feeling like Jonah in the belly of a fish: "A feeling like you are in the dark; alone, sopping wet, exhausted, and maybe even a bit nauseous."

So, if this is you, let's look at verses from Jonah chapter two. Jonah's own words paint quite a picture of being held by God in dire circumstances. After traveling almost two thousand miles in the opposite direction of his home, I'm sure Jonah just wants to get a glimpse of the proverbial soft white sand.

But instead, this is his reality:

You hurled me into the depths,
    into the very heart of the seas,
    and the currents swirled about me;
all your waves and breakers
    swept over me. . . .
The engulfing waters threatened me,
    the deep surrounded me;
    seaweed was wrapped around my head. (Jonah 2:3, 5 NIV)

And now, Jonah starts to see the soft white sand in his future, because he knows the Shepherd of the Sea by name.

To the roots of the mountains I sank down;
    the earth beneath barred me in forever.
But you, LORD my God,
    brought my life up from the pit. . . .
But I, with shouts of grateful praise,
    will sacrifice to you.
What I have vowed I will make good.
    I will say, "Salvation comes from the LORD." (Jonah 2:6,
      9 NIV)

I wonder if "the very heart of the seas" that Jonah mentions is the Abyss. While I have not experienced brown, curly seaweed wrapped around my head, I have, like you, experienced cruel currents swirling around me—the engulfing waves of the dark night of the soul. That quiet, ominous, often lonely feeling that overtakes us when we can't sleep in the middle of the night is a glimpse into this Abyss. For some people, this period lasts for months or years.

But even as time passes by in this ancient world, we are not alone. When we are treading water in the deep or we feel like we are about to drown, may we remember that the Shepherd of the Sea, the shepherd of our very soul, has never taken his eyes off us. Jonah shows us how he held the both/and in a three-day period. From fear to salvation. Shifting sands and changing tides. Our lives are like that too. The long hard seasons. The slippery passage of time. The ordinary weeks that turn into months where we think nothing is changing only to find one day the leaves on the trees have turned, much like the pages of our Kindle turning through a busy chapter.

As I sit and write in my sunroom, I'm used to the sun coming up as a rising fireball overhead—but in the darker months, the sun follows a different path toward the west all day. Things around us move and shift all the time, whether we notice it or not. By using nature as our guide, we can take on the steady but gradual movement we are offered.

Paradox

While it's never quite as linear as the sun traveling across the big blue sky, our rhythms, like the tide's ebb and flow, create the tempo and foundation for our days. Much of the time we get to choose if it's a slower out-to-sea rhythm or a speedboat-chase scenario. When we fly through the choppy waves, we tend to land harder. While smooth gliding is optimal, we know that slowing down is sometimes chosen for us. However, in our humanity, a shift to slower living always allows us to hold the paradox that is happening around us and within us. The hard and the soft. The grief and the joy. The agony and the laughter.

This paradox is a gift. Leaning into it instead of being afraid of conflicting feelings is part of letting yourself be human. The anticipation of eating the rich chocolate-peppermint pie at Christmas and also seeing the empty chair at the table. Savoring the chance to sit in the backyard with a book and a glass of sweet tea while also noticing the neighbors are at the beach for the week and you feel like the only one not on vacation. So many times, we experience these opposite emotions minutes or hours apart. Instead of fighting one emotion, making space for both feelings to coexist allows for true growth and empowerment. For ourselves and for others, to both be still and to flourish.

It's more than okay to do several of these things simultaneously today: Grieve, rest, celebrate, sing, pray, mourn, sleep, run, read, eat, cry, pause, walk, leave, smile, hug, sigh, feel sick, play, scream, linger, just be. Take a moment to think of a few words that come to you that feel opposite but true. In doing this exercise, you will see how slowing down to hold the both/and of the moment gives you a freedom to feel both the good and the bad. Holding

Instead of fighting one emotion, make space for both feelings to coexist.

space for your feelings and circumstances gives you authority to
move through them more gently and authentically.

When you or a loved one may long for the sight of soft white
sand in the distance, allow this breath prayer to gently carry you
to the shores of safety.

Breathe in: *"Though these deep waters are dark . . ."*
Breathe out: *"You are the Shepherd of the Sea."*

Here's to flying through the vast sea with you. As my friend Jen
says: don't forget to look up and look out. Hold the paradox in
your hands as you move through the deep, dark waters. While you
can barely see it on the horizon, another shift is coming.

For Reflection and Discussion

Where is your dark Abyss today?

If you see your stretch of soft white sand in the distance, are you
feeling expectant? What does it look like as it beckons you to safety?

What did you like best about the Breath Prayer listed above?

17

The Art of Letting Go

Leaving something doesn't need to leave a hole.
Sometimes it's necessary to lead to wholeness.
This means you get to move towards space, rest,
change, and the next place God wants to take
you. What a beautiful opportunity to trust.

HEATHER LOBE JOHNSON

WHAT'S YOUR FAVORITE EMOJI? Emoji are wonderful little symbols, aren't they? I use the palm tree emoji often, as it makes me smile and feel nostalgic. My friend Jill often uses the sheep and lion emoji when texting me as a reminder of Psalm 23 and Narnia. It might just be the modern way of communicating; and oh, how ironic that is.

Because, of course, communicating via picture is ancient. Growing up, one of my favorite Saturday morning excursions on the island happened when our family would take our little brown Suzuki jeep out to the remote area of Onima. Here we would take time to explore the Indian inscriptions on the limestone ledge of a low cave entrance. These red-stained symbols and designs were so intriguing to me. They've told stories since being created by the Arawak Indians back in the fifteenth century.

The first time I encountered a modern-day emoji, it was a little gift from God saying, "I see you." This was during one of the longest and hardest seasons of letting go that I have ever endured. I was newly widowed, stuck in my condo in Annapolis, Maryland, in the East Coast snowstorm of early 2000. I had a brand-new laptop and printer, my first one. On one of the days where all you could see out of every window was a never-ending white blanket of snow, my printer started making an abrupt noise. I walked over to the room where I had set it up to find a single sheet of paper coming out.

At first I wondered why a blank page would decide to print on its own. But then, I noticed it. A tiny, solitary black heart. I remember looking up, smiling through tears and saying "Thank you" to God for seeing me. In the months-long process of letting go of the only life I knew and starting a new one, God had sent me a symbol of love, reminding me that he was present. I was tethered to him through time and space.

These days, instead of hearing Queen Elsa of Arendelle's voice singing, "Let it go, let it go," I have instead been drawn over and over to the open hands emoji. It has many meanings: an invitation, a blessing, a form of querying, a prayer lifted high, and a symbol of the words—may it be so. A melting of our frozen frame of mind—open palms can feel like both a vulnerability and a welcomed truce.

Slow Living Shift
Releasing

I like to think of letting go more in terms of releasing, like a balloon or a dove—instead of detaching or disengaging. We cannot simply turn off our emotions and feelings when we begin letting go. But we can release the unnecessary burdens of time that others have placed on our shoulders. We can walk alongside people without carrying their heavy load. Heaviness does not get to cloak us in this season of reaching for the light.

Letting go is a process that starts in our hearts long before it moves down to our clenched hands that will be unfolding. One of the biggest reasons we cannot let go is because we don't know if we truly trust God. We want to have control so that if our prayers go unanswered, at least we ourselves have done all we can do.

One of the hardest things to do is to remove ourselves from something unhealthy—usually because it has become routine, it feels familiar, and we don't know what to do or where to go next. This could be releasing ties in a toxic relationship, leaving a high-pressure job without seeing what the future holds, or simply pausing something usually expected of you so that you can catch your breath and recover. It might mean letting go of a certain lifestyle and community to step out into the unknown while holding the hand of the One who knows you and sees what you need right now.

Letting go is a process that starts in our hearts long before it moves down to our clenched hands that will be unfolding.

Taking our hands off the proverbial wheel and submitting to God rarely seems to start well, but inevitably ends well. Sometimes I feel like I am not much different from my pets in this regard. When Dean and I started dating, my dog Rascal was a bit jealous. But he finally accepted Dean when their playful wrestling turned Rascal's defensive stance into a happy belly-up posture. A posture that feels scary and freeing all at the same time. A relinquishing of sorts, when we need to stay tethered to our Master for safety and provision, knowing in our gut that we weren't meant to do it alone. Whatever your "it" happens to be—this stance of open hands slowly helps shift our doubt, fear, and hesitation.

Some Things to Consider

- Be gentle with yourself through this process—no need to wish you were stronger, as you will soon realize how strong you have become through this occurrence.
- Take care of yourself through solid self-care and soul care—our bodies need extra sleep, food, water, and the gentle presence of others right now.
- Move more slowly than you think you are allowed to—this might look like asking for time off a job or obligations instead of plowing through.
- Talk with a safe person in your life about this season—this might be a spiritual director, a best friend, or a licensed therapist.
- Journal your stream of thought—when journaling, write, type, or voice text what comes to your mind at that very moment; your brain is processing this shifting and it's okay to not know how you really feel about your circumstances; this isn't the time to document what you think you should be learning during this season.

Part of releasing is letting go of things that aren't helpful anymore, so don't be surprised if you do some unlearning during this pivotal time. This release is hard and healthy inner work. I am here to tell you that you can let it take as long as it takes. Some things aren't meant to happen fast. But rest assured that healing happens silently in the steadfast slowness and the necessary unraveling as we hold our hands open in hope.

I particularly love how Shauna Niequist blends delight in with letting go as she enters what she refers to as a new "delight era." It helps me shift my thinking to remember that letting go can be a sweet thing and not always dreadful. On Instagram, Shauna says, "What do I *really* want? I want joy. And dancing. And beauty. And play. Lightness of spirit. Letting go, as often as necessary. Choosing peace. Belonging to myself. Walking away from about a million things I didn't need after all. . . . Delight. Delight. Delight."

The practice of letting go starts to build our trust in God in a greater way. Something starts relaxing in us and gives us a quiet peace where we are resolved to listen to that still small voice more often. It can also become easier for us to open our eyes, and then open our hands, as we see someone else's need.

Recently, I had a vulnerable and beautiful encounter upon meeting a new friend. We were standing with our mutual friend Sarah when I noticed Lauren's earrings moving as she talked. I asked her if I could see them. As she took her hand and brushed her hair out of the way, there were the prettiest dangling nautical shells ever. They looked just like the symbol on the spine of some of my favorite books! InterVarsity Press's Formatio imprint is symbolized with the spiral of a nautilus, a representation of the

deep inward work of spiritual formation. My eyes started filling
with tears as I nodded to Sarah, who understood the irony of the
symbol. As I stood there, I started to see how God had brought
my life full circle.

What Lauren did not know is that I had signed a book contract
earlier that summer with InterVarsity Press—a dream I have held
close for many years.

What both Sarah and Lauren did not know was that I have a
massive white nautilus shell that was handed down to me from
my grandmother; it's been sitting in my writing spaces for years
now. It's a symbol of my grandparents' slow living days in Florida,
where they would walk the shoreline, go fishing, eat meals with
friends, and practice a slower, gentler pace several months out of
the year. My grandmother died at age ninety-eight, and this shell
is over five decades old.

Looking back, what I did not know was that God would in-
tensify my passion for inviting others to live slowly. He would give
me gifts like the shell and other beautiful symbols to encourage
me along the journey to publishing.

While my mind was putting pieces of God's tangible goodness
together, Lauren started taking her earrings off. She handed them
to me, saying that they didn't belong to her anymore. They were
for me, and she wanted me to have them.

At that moment, I felt God's care for me in such a palpable
way. God used Lauren, who, I found out much later, was actively
implementing the art of releasing, to show me that he saw me.
Lauren never even hesitated to let go of her earrings and give
them to me, a stranger. We never know when we are participating
with God in the healing or joy of another person. But it starts with

open hands. May you, too, have a Lauren experience of your own if you haven't already.

Becoming Our Driftwood Selves

As a young child, my favorite place to plop down in my dirt yard was in the massive piece of driftwood that I called my boat. It was more like a fat canoe; however, its slow transformation from, most likely, a large dead tree to a decorative play toy seemed epic. This battered piece of wood was the centerpiece of our front yard, and there was a round little seat hollowed out by nature where I would sit to watch a car, bicyclist, or pedestrian pass by.

Driftwood was something I came across on a regular basis. Sometimes on Saturdays my family would go out to the "rough side" of the island, driving past the Trans World Radio site where the radio transmitters were housed.

We would walk along the gray, rocky edge, safely staying in front of where the waves pounded the jagged rocks and washed up all matter of interesting things. A massive amount of driftwood along with debris would scatter the coastline. A single orange flip-flop, a buoy, and an empty and sun-bleached dish soap bottle were always part of the landscape it seemed. Such a 180-degree difference in scenery from the opposite side of our island where the white sandy beaches lay and the turquoise waters housed the pristine calm reefs.

And thinking of all the driftwood I saw over the years, I wonder . . . maybe instead of striving to make everything constantly look and feel just right or fully restored, could we embrace the past, present, and future? It's what makes us who we are. Pain, scars, sadness, joy, beauty, breath, memories. Holding hope and holding space for all of it in the becoming.

Some of the most profound writing I have read to this day is from writer Beth Mabe Gianopulos, who shares her family's experience at Driftwood Beach in Georgia. I find myself a bit envious of the tangible way that nature could "hold space" and "release" during these experiences, as well as envious of Beth herself in the middle of such beauty. On this beach, a strange light shone, illuminating the proximity of how God sees us and how we can see others through pain and transformation.

Beth says:

Sun-bleached trees tiredly stood in the sand reaching furtively for the sky. Twisting limbs and fallen trees were scattered haphazardly across the sand, moving ever so slightly as the dark blue waves slowly receded. As the tide rolled back, white stumps slowly rose from the ocean like ghosts of a time past. It was like stepping into another world or another time. . . .

The beach was eerie—a scene clouded with chaos and death. Huge trees that had once stood proudly were shadows of their former selves. The vibrant greens and browns were leached away, leaving wood that was white and bleached by the salty waves and sun. Yet, I did not feel overcome by the chaos and the death. When I looked closer at the trees, I discovered that they were teeming with life. Tiny snails and anemones covered the trunks and branches. The beach evoked every emotion at once—awe, sadness, wonder, loss, and hope. Death and life entwined together in a delicate dance in this holy place. It was one of the most hauntingly beautiful places that I have ever been.

Like the weathered, bare-rooted, scattered, twisted chunks of driftwood, gorgeous in their own right, I have in recent years begun to understand that like a good movie, each segment holds an important part of what makes that story unique and even whole. When a chapter in our life closes, we don't usually look the way we originally did. So much has changed. But we have to let go to keep moving forward, grateful that we are here. We are more weathered and more wise. Let the light show that we have lived through letting go of what we cannot keep, and that we are now even more alive.

Let the light show that we have lived through letting go of what we cannot keep, and that we are now even more alive.

Can we feel fulfilled in who we are becoming? Can we eventually be content by releasing who we have been? May we be satisfied with our driftwood selves, knowing that God restores and remakes the broken pieces in his timing, not ours. The slow-but-necessary unfolding and remaking bear the marks of a life fully lived.

For Reflection and Discussion

Consider a posture of both offering and receiving: cupping your hands together, palms upward. What comes to mind?

What are ways you can envision letting go and releasing in a way that takes the dread out of it and makes it more bearable?

If someone has shown you God's love and kindness through their own letting go of something, what was that? How did it impact you?

18

Resting in the Belief That We Are Truly Held

Remember, you are held safe. You are loved.
You are protected. You are in communion with
God and with those whom God has sent you.
What is of God will last. It belongs to the eternal
life. Choose it, and it will be yours.

Henri J. M. Nouwen

WHILE I WAS ATTENDING a spiritual formation retreat called the Apprentice Gathering, held in Wichita, Kansas, in the fall of 2019, God gave me the sweet gift to see a bit more of my own story. Apparently, I have struggled with completely trusting God. It's possible you've felt similarly now or in the past; through bits of conversation with friends and peers, I have come to understand that this is not at all uncommon.

I believe in God. I love God. I even look back to the many ways my Creator has been faithful to me over the decades. But somewhere along the years I tried to take back the control and hold the reins tighter than ever, seeking to keep more pieces of my life from falling apart. I would even mutter clichés I didn't believe, like

"These things happen for a reason." Maybe to convince myself? I don't really know. Like a young child, wrangling in his mother's arms despite her kind face and warm embrace, my heart would often flail about, feeling unsettled, out of sync.

Slow Living Shift
Believing We're Held and Resting in That Knowledge

Far from home, sitting in this old 1920s chapel, in a sacred place called Friends University, with golden hour streaming through the pink and orange hues of the stained-glass windows, I started to understand certain roots of my fear and unsettledness. It was all well and good that I had found, and even taught others, ways to bring island living into busy suburban lives. It was fulfilling to engage in deep conversations with women from all walks of life where we agreed on the importance of thriving, rest, how much our people mattered, the nourishment of soul care, and the stability of anchoring in for those hard times.

But one more thing had been missing this whole time. Of all the ways I was learning to enjoy life, content with my people and as my true self, I didn't have the completely settled feeling with *God* that I was desiring. I couldn't put my finger on it but knew in my gut it wasn't there.

Singing the old hymn "How Great Thou Art" in unison with four hundred people in this chapel brought me back to singing the hymn in church as a missionary kid. I think God was setting the stage for something that day as the words washed over me. I had a feeling that this spiritual formation trip would bring some beautiful healing my way. Sometimes God ushers in answers via the most unexpected places and down-to-earth people.

On our last afternoon at Friends University, I ran up to talk to William Paul Young, one of our keynote speakers, as he was getting in his rental car. Paul wrote a book called *The Shack*. Maybe you've heard of it. Over the years, when anyone asked me if I had read Paul's book, I would always just shrug it off. But somewhere in my gut, I knew that I just didn't want to go there—I was afraid I would have too many similarities with the main character. And I didn't want to go deeper into a pain I thought I had worked so hard to emerge from. So, I had never read the book. (And I told Paul that.) But during this trip, some truths became clear to me. Over the span of those three days in retreat, I spent valuable time with my people—soul sisters and soul brothers—as we unpacked our lives and contemplated deep spiritual formation.

Here's where I realized that refusing to slow down came from a deep fear of having to decide what I thought about the goodness of God. During his keynote sessions, Paul shared wisdom from his own times of suffering, "The truth is that our hearts are actually drawn to God. But in fear, we'd rather have religion than Trust. And that makes it hard to declare the goodness of God." To understand how much God loves us, Paul said we should imagine God gently saying to us, "I am especially fond of you." He also said something profound that speaks to an age-old battle in our human minds, "Until you believe that God is good, you'll never trust him." When he said that, something deep inside of me started to emerge from the grave. I knew that *that* was the struggle I'd had for many years after the horrific accident, then eventual death of my first husband, Brian. Trust. Did I really trust God? No, I did not.

In my awakening that day, it felt good to come clean with someone, although I never imagined I'd be coming clean to a famous author approaching the car that would take him to the airport. My friend Gem had encouraged me to walk over. I am thankful for her own spiritual work in areas like resistance and vulnerability—maybe she sensed that I needed to do this. There is a deep sense of relief when we can finally put words to our wrestling hearts.

Did I really trust God? No, I did not.

My voice cracked as I explained to Paul how God had just graciously used some of the backstory from his writing of *The Shack* to draw me into a deeper part of my pain and then ease it. It hit me that the reason I finally have so much peace in these last few years is because I finally, unequivocally know and believe that not only is God good but that *I am held.* That *you are held.* Through the pain and the unanswered questions. Through the feelings many of us have but are too afraid to whisper to someone else. And we can rest in that knowledge, which is at the center of a spiritual slowing down.

* * *

My spiritual director, Maeve, who you met earlier in the book, recently pointed out to me that when describing my spiritual life and my place in this world, I've begun to use the word *settled.* Do I wish I had this understanding of God in my late twenties when my life took an ugly turn instead of in my early fifties, when I feel like my soul is weathered? Of course. All of us have regrets about the time that has vanished. We wonder what life would have been like if we had seen more clearly or trusted more deeply. But this wrestling we go through is holy work. It is not to be rushed or glossed over. These are the life rhythms that we must learn to glide on, like riding out a wave. We can literally exhale with thankful hearts because God pursues us our whole life.

A lot of solitude and sitting still with God, in my little sunroom, took place before this trip to Wichita ever happened. There were times I felt lonely and wondered what I was supposed to be asking or doing in, for instance, my relationships, my writing life, my health, and my church. Some of my spiritual questions seemed to loom over me like a rain cloud. Where was my sunshine? Where was my soft white island sand?

I shouldn't be surprised that God brought me to Kansas to fill in an unanswered piece of my story, should I? I'm guessing you've experienced a part of your story being written in a way you least expected too. Perhaps you've had your own wrestling while sitting in a pew under beautiful stained-glass windows: being reminded of the broken beauty of life and its restoration that almost seems tangible. Where was your wrestling? Was it a long time ago? Was it recently?

So, yes, God is good. But he is also *with* us. That's what Emmanuel means. A word we can carry with us every season of our one precious life. We have an attachment to our heavenly Father, to the Shepherd of the Sea, that no one can rip us away from. Sometimes God's goodness is illuminated and sometimes it's hidden in the darkness, despite our best efforts to understand our circumstances.

How is your heart today? It's fine to sit with God in this un-comfortable wrestling for as long as you need to. He is with you. And because he is with you, you are most definitely being held. Dwelling in the goodness of God is a theme for our weary days. Hold on to that and sink into this deep invitation, my friend!

Resting in the Knowledge that You Are Held

One of the deepest and most profound benefits of a slowed-down life is finally resting in the knowledge that you are not alone, you are seen, and you are truly being held. It's a peace that your body and your mind know is true. But until that happens, there is no shame in telling God, just like the grieving father told Jesus, "I believe; help my unbelief" (Mark 9:24 ESV). The Good News Translation says it like this: "The father at once cried out: 'I do have faith, but not enough. Help me have more!'"

Once we grasp this freedom, we become settled, and that rhythm of slow, out-to-sea drifting sets the tone for the rest of our days—just like men in the "banana boats" I saw on many walks to the pier so long ago with my mother. They were being held in snug hammocks while rocking high above loads of banana cargo. This is God's overarching embrace of humankind: being held by the Creator of the Universe.

These lyrics in the song "Empires," from the debut album by C'est Lis, capture the heart of this deep trust that allows us to truly slow down and accept God's love: "To be settled is to be seen. To surrender is to receive."

In my preparation to conclude this chapter, I, like Moses in the Old Testament, have had to rely on friends to figuratively hold my own arms up for me when this journey has been tiring, when

I didn't know if my words would matter, and when my own weary questions still lingered. But I can trust in the words of safe, strong friends—the friends God chose for me. Jill told me to move into the story of acceptance in the Beloved. Jen told me to go deeper. And finally, Maeve instructed me to "swim out further—over the turquoise line to the Abyss." She wanted me to remember to "not hold back the ways we show up in the world" as I put these words onto paper for me and for you.

This shift to slow living is such a process, and yet we don't have to walk it alone. It is accomplished not all at once but one step at a time. It is a beautiful journey of looking back to see the fingerprints of God's faithfulness all through your story, because all along it's been *his* story. As my husband Dean has recently reminded me, "Nothing can happen outside of his plan, because we're part of his plan." God walks with us through the unanswered questions and sends friends to keep us company in our wonderings and wanderings. They comfort, listen, and then spur us onward.

These almost twenty chapters of sheer vulnerability have been years in the making. But I never dreamed that writing this book would slow me down even further to sit with more questions. It has compelled me to decide what I truly believe about God and about myself. God's coming beside me—in the joyful times, in the dark times, when slowing down has been chosen for me, and in the times of holding tension—has solidified my trust in his goodness, kindness, and nearness. His faithfulness is all around us, but we often have to look back to see it.

The Day I Could Finally Exhale

Do not be surprised if God mixes science, emotions, and therapy together as he heals your broken heart.

In the last few years, God took a deep pain I had experienced over twenty-five years ago and invited me to finally surrender it to him. It happened when someone who could have been attentive to me chose to dismiss me. This was the morning that Brian died, before family and friends had gotten to our house yet.

I went to this person to give and receive a hug, but they put their hands up to let me know they would not touch me in my shock and grief. Standing there, I knew that except for my dog, Rascal, who was standing on the back deck, I was truly alone. This utter loneliness lasted almost two hours before my people started arriving. I felt confused and angry. I longed for a safe embrace.

Fast-forward to just three years ago, through an EMDR session with my therapist, when I started to slowly let go of the hurt from this rejection. I started to see that this person was hurting as much as I was; it wasn't all about me.

And finally, last year, in God's kindness, he gave me a vision. I was once again standing in front of this person who had dismissed me in some of the most painful hours of my life—when all of a sudden, I saw Jesus standing between us to soften the blow and give me the safe embrace I had needed twenty-five years prior. He wrapped me in his arms in a warm hug. My pain started to melt after more than two decades of holding in this bitterness.

But then, to my utter surprise, I watched as Jesus turned to face and embrace this person who had hurt me. And he acknowledged and healed their pain as well. At that moment, I knew that God's love was tangible and was freely given, not only to me but to every other person around me—regardless of what I had thought of them. I felt the Holy Spirit confirm that I indeed did want Jesus to love even my enemies equally. The vision solidified a much deeper belief that God is good and does not have favorites. A clear message that I was held. You are held.

A peace came over me like never before. *This was when my peace was solidified, and I could truly and finally exhale.* What a slow journey of trust, reliance, and ultimately accepting the gift of rest, and the full knowledge of being held. May we not be fearful of what we will find when we accept God's kind invitation to slow down.

As we've spent this time together, has something surfaced for you that you find yourself now wrestling with? Come with open hands to God, asking him to help you believe. I think we all know by now that this shift to slow living isn't about sitting on the couch and eating bonbons. It's about naming our story, identifying our capacity, practicing ordinary soul care, living face to face in deeper ways, creating the time and space to hear the still small voice, being fully present, and standing up for ourselves.

When we started out in this book together, I saw your beautiful, tired face. And now, I want you to look up into the eyes of the One who so deeply loves you as you realize that the gaze holding your face belongs to the Shepherd of the Sea. He longs for you to know that he is standing face to face with you. He sees you just as you are and just as you are becoming.

Believing we are held is what holds our story together like the binding on this book. I want to leave you with the same invitation that Maeve gave me in a recent spiritual direction session. It's the very first line from the poem "Patient Trust," written by Pierre

> *Above all, trust in the slow work of God.*
>
> PIERRE TEILHARD DE CHARDIN

Teilhard de Chardin as found in Nancy Bieber's book, *Decision Making and Spiritual Discernment*. "Above all, trust in the slow work of God."

Return to the salty island air with me; not for a vacation from our life, but for the purpose of walking each other home. Let it awaken, refresh, and even heal you in the most profound way. May you exhale today. May you relish in living slowly.

For Reflection and Discussion

There is no shame in saying that you aren't sure if you fully trust God. Is there something holding you back?

What does it feel like to rest in the knowledge that you are held? What does it feel like to know that the Shepherd of the Sea is always standing watch?

Can you slow down, knowing that he never takes his gaze off you? Are you ready to start your own shift to slower living?

BENEDICTION

As your day ebbs and flows
May you rest in the fact that your
life is not an assembly line.
While the world around
you grinds and screeches
May you linger in the smooth,
quieter rhythms that give you life.
As you hold and ponder your own
difficult and joyful obligations
May you give yourself time
and space to process it all.
As you look within, as you look
around, and as you look up
May a slower, more deliberate
pace cause you to be kinder
and more fully present to
yourself and others.

Acknowledgments

THIS BOOK HAS THE SOUL PRINTS of so many lovely people woven through the pages. I couldn't have written it without the support and input of my beloved community helping me bring this invitation of slower living into the world.

Dr. Bhavna Vaidya, Dr. Amelia Kelley, Dr. Keith Dockery, Ruth, Scarlet, Rona, Juliette, Patty, Ann, Ariel, Sheila, Laura, Heather, Amber, Brandy, Menda, Alison, Amy, Diane, Patti, Christie, Bekah, Vina, Joon, Sue, Katie, Mariel, Lex, Jenai, Ronne, Tracy, AR, Lillie, Elisa, JDL, Margot, Lori, Lore, KSP, Sherry, Cary, Twyla, Tounes, Tami, Annelies, Dave and Becky, Shawn and Maile, KJ and Ryan, Gem and Alan, Kevin and Melanie, Caleb and Ana, our local Writers Mixer, and my friends from TWR and Bonaire—thanks for your kindness and support!

Mary DeMuth—you're a beautiful gift to the world. Grateful you're my friend and agent!

Debbie Alsdorf—thanks for your friendship as my agent at Books & Such.

Cindy Bunch—I'm so delighted you saw my vision for *Live Slowly* from the beginning. Thanks for your kindness and wisdom. You're a treasured editor and friend who has generously turned this book into a beautiful offering of words for our dear readers.

Lori Neff, Krista Clayton, David Fassett, Amanda, Allie, and the team—you are greatly appreciated!

InterVarsity Press—thanks for partnering with me and believing in my words. You do incredible work bringing good books into the world. I'm honored mine has found its home.

A big thank you to my endorsers! Your own work inspires me greatly. It is a gift that you believe in this book—you're amazing partners.

Cheryl Eichman, Honey Wiggs, Kenny and Kim Latimore, Jenny Pollock, GACC and Life Group friends: Ann and Bruce, Marilyn, Vickie, Kevin and Maura—thanks for being friends who've continually prayed for me while I wrote this book.

Richella Parham, Cary Brege, Lindsay Stevenson, Jennifer Slenk, Megan Gardner, Amy Carroll, and Kara Yuza—you each bring such joy to my life, impacting me personally and professionally. Grateful for your trusted friendships.

Karen Benson, Jennie Voliva, Missy Brookeshire, and Kate Perry—you've known and loved me for two decades of this Carolina living. So overwhelmingly grateful for you.

Summer Gross, Maeve Gerboth, Kris Camealy, Julianne Clayton, and Bette Dickinson—my contemplative soul care sisters. I'm blessed to call you very dear friends. Summer, my writing sojourner, and Maeve, my spiritual director—thank you for continuously coming alongside me.

Aundi Kolber, Emily P. Freeman, Natasha Smith, Sarah Westfall, and Prasanta Verma—your integrity, care, and friendship mean so much. It's an honor to write alongside you!

Lissa Wertz, Lynn Faggion, and Heather MacAulay—I'm in debt to you for showing me what sisters-in-Christ look like. Our years of deep friendship, trips, and coffee dates are irreplaceable.

Jennifer Bleakley—thanks for your faithfulness. You're such a beautiful and treasured friend. And one day we shall sit on a tropical beach somewhere toasting to the writing life.

Jill Grouse—God has been so kind to bring you, Greg, Aaron, and Meredith into our lives. Love you so, my best friend. We are two sheep who know we are seen and held by God.

Brian, Nancy, and Vickie—I love you. I deeply cherish the short but precious years we had together. You'll always be family.

Sue, Buddy, Bob, Darlene, Cody, Dawn, Todd, Jessica, Danny, Kristin, Caroline, and Caleb—I'm so glad to be in the Grubbs family! Thank you for your care and support. Love you all.

Sherri, John, Ian, and Reikr—love you guys! Thankful for family.

Roger and Carolyn—I treasure your deep love and daily prayers throughout the years, Mom and Dad. You've been steadfast through my joys and sorrows. Love you!

Lili—I'm so happy to be your mom. You enrich my life. Thankful God gave you to us, our beautiful, brilliant daughter. Love you so much.

Dean—I'm so proud to be your wife. Grateful for your love, discernment, support, and partnership. I love you! Here's to many more years together. #ourislandinthecity

Shepherd of the Sea—I am beyond grateful to you, oh God. Your love has held me this whole time. Great is thy faithfulness.

The Slow Living Shifts

Slow Living Shifts *for each chapter*

1. exhaling
2. acceptance
3. restoration and reflection
4. embracing your uniqueness
5. understanding capacity
6. awakening to beauty
7. sustainable rhythms
8. soul care practices
9. finding sanctuary
10. savoring
11. seeking out solitude
12. lingering with intention
13. being present to others
14. being empowered
15. boundaries in faith settings
16. expectancy
17. releasing
18. believing we're held and resting in that knowledge

Group Discussion Guide

You can use the questions found at the end of each chapter in order to create a group discussion experience. Here's a possible structure to use for six weeks, consisting of one-hour sessions.

Week One

Preparation before meeting:
- Read the introduction, chapter one, and chapter two.
- Highlight or write down the SLOW acronym from the introduction.

Discussion while meeting:
- Discuss the questions from the three chapters above.
- There's a difference between choosing to live slowly and being forced to slow down. Share your experiences, and give an example of being slowed down or not being in control.
- Contemplate Frederick Buechner's quote at the end of chapter two to close out your discussion.

Week Two

Preparation before meeting:
- Read chapters three through six.
- Contemplate this desperate need in our society to slow down and exhale.

Discussion while meeting:
- Discuss the questions from the four chapters above.
- Share your thoughts on slowing down and exhaling.
- Use the Benediction after chapter six to close out your discussion.

Week Three

Preparation before meeting:

- Read chapters seven through ten.
- Think about how learning to slow down can play out for you this year.

Discussion while meeting:

- Discuss the questions from the four chapters above.
- Share which Slow Living Shift from these chapters you will focus on.
- As you finish, read and contemplate together the meaning of the epigraph by Matthew Kelly in chapter eight.

Week Four

Preparation before meeting:

- Read chapters eleven through thirteen.
- Contemplate the benefits of solitude, a lingering pace, and being fully present.

Discussion while meeting:

- Discuss the questions from the three chapters above.
- Share about a time when you've experienced solitude.
- Use the Benediction after chapter thirteen to close out your discussion.

Week Five

Preparation before meeting:

- Read chapters fourteen and fifteen.
- Ask yourself if you believe that you are indeed free to live slowly.

Discussion while meeting:

- Discuss the questions from the two chapters above.
- Share which Slow Living Shift from these chapters you will focus on.
- Consider the phrase "I'm going to have to pass. Thank you." See how that feels as you close out your discussion.

Week Six

Preparation before meeting:

- Read chapters sixteen through eighteen.
- Contemplate what you can let go of in order to fully exhale.

Discussion while meeting:

- Discuss the questions from the three chapters above.
- Share an aspect of trusting God that you've worked through as you contemplate "trusting in the slow work of God."
- Use the Closing Benediction after chapter eighteen to close out your discussion.

Notes

Introduction: A Return to Everyday Island Living

4 *John's note says*: John Ortberg, *Soul Keeping: Caring for the Most Important Part of You* (Grand Rapids, MI: Zondervan, 2014), 93.

5 *Little by little*: Quoted in Cliff Michaels, *The 4 Essentials: A Misfit's Journey to Mindset, Strategies, Values & Purpose* (Thousand Oaks, CA: Cliff Michaels Global Learning, 2016), 90.

1. When Sea Breeze and Road Rage Collide

14 *Feeling the need to be busy*: Tutu Mora, "Participating in the culture," Instagram, June 28, 2019, www.instagram.com/p/BzQXmbFnlb0/.

17 *This is where our obsession*: Carl Honoré, *In Praise of Slow: Challenging the Cult of Speed* (San Francisco: HarperOne, 2004), 13.

2. Sometimes Slowing Down Is Chosen for You

22 *Embrace uncertainty*: Bob Goff, Twitter post, October 28, 2014, https://twitter.com/bobgoff/status/527113753746477058?lang=en.

25 *Tell me what it is:* Mary Oliver, "The Summer Day," printed in Judith Valente and Charles Reynard, *Twenty Poems to Nourish Your Soul* (Chicago: Loyola Press, 2005), 3.

27 *Laura not only:* Portions of chapter two appeared as a blog post in *The Uncommon Normal*, "When You Can't Pay It Back or Pay It Forward," April 28, 2022, https://theuncommonnormal.com/what-if-i-cant-pay-it-forward/.

29 *Listen to your life*: Frederick Buechner, *Listening to Your Life: Daily Meditations with Frederick Buechner* (New York: HarperCollins, 2009), 9.

3. A Sea Glass Transformation

32 *Like us, sea glass:* Mary Beth Beuke (owner of www.westcoastseaglass.com), personal correspondence on July 3, 2023.

35 *It was A. W. Tozer who said:* A. W. Tozer, *The Pursuit of God* (Harrisburg, PA: Christian Publications, Inc., 2011), 31, Kindle.

36   *We move at the pace:* Gem and Alan Fadling, *What Does Your Soul Love? Eight Questions That Reveal God's Work in You* (Downers Grove, IL: InterVarsity Press, 2019), 14.

      Sea glass takes several decades: "Sea Glass," Wikipedia article, accessed 26 April 2023, https://en.wikipedia.org/wiki/Sea_glass.

4. You Are Exactly Who You Are Supposed to Be

41   *Someone who has:* Andre Sólo and Jenn Granneman, "What Is a Highly Sensitive Person?," Highly Sensitive Refuge, https://highlysensitiverefuge.com /what-is-highly-sensitive-person/.

42   *One in five people:* Elaine Aron, *The Highly Sensitive Person: How to Thrive When the World Overwhelms You* (New York: Harmony/Rodale, 1997), 6.

43   *Whether out of love or self-preservation:* Clint Watkins, Instagram post, June 29, 2021, www.instagram.com/p/CQtGlPxNPeU/.

44   *You come home:* Hoda Kotb, *This Just Speaks to Me: Words to Live By Every Day* (New York: Penguin, 2020), 33.

      A third to a half: Susan Cain, "The Power of Introverts," TED talk, March 2, 2012, https://www.ted.com/talks/susan_cain_the_power_of_introverts /c/transcript.

45   *Is quite common:* "No Workplace Is Immune to Invisible Illness and Hidden Health Issues," *Paytient* blog, October 18, 2022, www.paytient.com/blog /no-workplace-is-immune-to-invisible-illness-and-hidden-health-issues.

47   *We are invited to cease:* Aundi Kolber, *Try Softer: A Fresh Approach to Move Us Out of Anxiety, Stress, and Survival Mode—and Into a Life of Connection and Joy* (Carol Stream, IL: Tyndale House, 2020), 110.

5. Understanding Capacity

50   *The rapid advancement:* Eric Niiler, "How the Second Industrial Revolution Changed Americans' Lives," History.com, updated July 25, 2023, www .history.com/news/second-industrial-revolution-advances.

6. Awakening to Beauty

62   *Transformed dive tourism:* Tom Morrisey, "The Legends and Heroes of Scuba Diving," *Sport Diver*, April 21, 2006, www.sportdiver.com/keywords /living-legends/living-legends.

63   *When the sun sets for the day:* Chetana Babburjung Purushotham, "Life After Dark: The Night Shift on a Coral Reef," *RoundGlass Sustain*, May 12, 2022, https://roundglasssustain.com/wildvaults/night-coral-reef.

65   *These benefits:* "How the Brain Is Affected by Art," American Congress of Rehabilitation Medicine (blog), accessed February 1, 2023, https://acrm.org /rehabilitation-medicine/how-the-brain-is-affected-by-art/.

7. Rhythms for Sunrise to Sunset

71 *Take the first step:* Attributed to Martin Luther King by Marion Wright Edelman, "Kids First," *Mother Jones* 16, no. 31 (May-June 1991), 77.

75 *Use the Daily Office:* The rest of this chapter will describe the Daily Office in greater depth. This fixed time of prayer typically consists of a short and ordered time of silence, Scripture, a devotional, a question to contemplate, a prayer to read, and ending in silence again.

77 *My favorite book:* Peter Scazzero, *Emotionally Healthy Spirituality Day by Day: A 40-Day Journey with the Daily Office* (Grand Rapids, MI: Zondervan, 2014).

8. Soul Care for a Slowed-Down Life

82 *The final joy:* Quoted in Tim Challies, *Knowing and Enjoying God* (Eugene, OR: Harvest House Publishers, 2021), 45.

83 *Spiritual direction is a counter-cultural practice:* Emily P. Freeman, "The Art and Practice of Spiritual Direction," Emily P. Freeman website, https://emilypfreeman.com/spiritualdirection.

86 *That simple prayer:* Jennifer Tucker, *Breath as Prayer: Calm Your Anxiety, Focus Your Mind, and Renew Your Soul* (Nashville: Thomas Nelson, 2022), 18-19.

9. Where's Your Island in the City?

95 *Nicole says:* To hear more from Nicole, see Jodi Grubbs, "The Spiritual Practice of Celebration with Nicole Zasowski," June 7, 2022, in *Our Island in the City,* podcast, https://podcasts.apple.com/us/podcast/the-spiritual-practice-of-celebration-with/id1494249906?i=1000565484736.

10. Savoring, One Sip at a Time

102 *Nothing is missing:* Quantrilla Ard, PhD, "Y'all! Things already look differently," Instagram, January 3, 2023, www.instagram.com/p/Cm9__iRv2_u/?utm_source=ig_web_copy_link&igshid=MzRlODBiNWFlZA==.

103 *"El Domino":* Captain Tim, "Puerto Rico Dominoes Rules," *Caribbean Trading Company* blog, September 25, 2012, https://caribbeantrading.com/dominoes-rules-in-puerto-rico/.

104 *As I walk:* Prasanta Verma, "The Feast of Friendship," *The Mudroom,* November 29, 2022, https://mudroomblog.com/the-feast-of-friendship/.

105 *A rooted and nostalgic exercise:* George Ella Lyon, "Where I'm From, a Poem by George Ella Lyon," personal blog, 2010, www.georgeellalyon.com/where.html.

107 *So often I spin:* Summer Gross, "Spiritual Practice of a Summer Day," June 27, 2019, in *The Presence Project,* podcast, https://podcasts.apple.com/us/podcast/spiritual-practice-of-a-summer-day/id1462343703?i=1000442951283.

108   *The sea does not reward:* Anne Morrow Lindbergh, *Gift from the Sea* (New York: Knopf Doubleday, 1991), 144.

11. Solitude and Spaciousness

113   *Loneliness creates a void:* Anna Rachel Bolch, personal correspondence on January 24, 2023.

115   *Relaxing is allowing:* Jodi Grubbs, "The Benefits of a Personal Quarterly Retreat," with Carla H. Hayden, in *Our Island in the City,* podcast, August 3, 2021, https://podcasts.apple.com/us/podcast/our-island-in-the-city-podcast/id1494249906?i=1000530853281.

116   *I live in that solitude:* Quoted in *The Handbook of Solitude: Psychological Perspectives on Social Isolation, Social Withdrawal, and Being Alone* (Hoboken, NJ: Wiley, 2014), 93.

        Our brains simply aren't: Jane Porter, "How Solitude Can Change Your Brain in Profound Ways," *Fast Company*, October 15, 2016, www.fastcompany.com/3052061/how-solitude-can-change-your-brain-in-profound-ways.

12. A Lingering Pace with God and Others

121   *God in himself is a sweet society:* Richella Parham, *Mythical Me: Finding Freedom from Constant Comparison* (Downers Grove, IL: InterVarsity Press, 2019), 42.

122   *When we engage the Scriptures:* Ruth Haley Barton, *Sacred Rhythms: Arranging Our Lives for Spiritual Transformation* (Downers Grove, IL: InterVarsity Press, 2009), 50.

        And he walks with me: C. Austin Miles, "In the Garden" (hymn), 1912.

123   *We may ignore:* C. S. Lewis, *Letters to Malcolm: Chiefly on Prayer* (London, UK: Geoffrey Bles, 1964), 75.

13. Barefoot Hospitality Means Being Present

131   *When the Lord does:* Jodi Grubbs, "Conversation with Spiritual Director Summer Joy Gross," in *Our Island in the City,* podcast, June 15, 2020, https://podcasts.apple.com/us/podcast/conversation-with-spiritual-director-summer-joy-gross/id1494249906?i=1000478127702.

        When we listen, we invite others: Adam S. McHugh, *The Listening Life: Embracing Attentiveness in a World of Distraction* (Downers Grove, IL: InterVarsity Press, 2015), 25.

132   *Pasture Experience Retreat:* For more information, see www.pastureexperience.com.

138   *Silver and gold:* Joseph V. Micallef, "The Surprising Story of Bonaire's Salt Pyramids," *Forbes*, April 18, 2019, www.forbes.com/sites/joemicallef/2019/04/18/the-surprising-story-of-bonaires-salt-pyramids/?sh=53e87ea76adf.

14. You've Had Permission All Along

146   *If we want to live:* Brené Brown, *The Gifts of Imperfection: Let Go of Who You Think You're Supposed to Be and Embrace Who You Are* (Center City, MN: Hazelden, 2010), 144.

148   *Relational intelligence is the ability*: Dharius Daniels, *Relational Intelligence: The People Skills You Need for the Life of Purpose You Want* (Grand Rapids, MI: Zondervan, 2020), 15.

17. The Art of Letting Go

179   *What do I really want:* Shauna Niequist, "My relationship with resolutions," Instagram, January 3, 2023, www.instagram.com/p/Cm9jThMOdEo/?igshid =MzRlODBiNWFlZA%3D%3D, and personal correspondence with author on January 6, 2023.

182   *Sun-bleached trees:* Beth Gianopulos, "Driftwood on the Sand," *Everyday Exiles* blog, September 28, 2017, https://everydayexiles.com/driftwood-on-the -sand/. Additional personal correspondence on July 4, 2023.

18. Resting in the Belief That We Are Truly Held

187   *During his keynote sessions:* Author's notes from William Paul Young, keynote lectures at The Apprentice Gathering, Wichita, KS, September 26–28, 2019. Personal correspondence with author on September 6, 2023.

190   *To be settled:* "Empires," written by Elisa Cox, track 1 on C'est Lis, *Empires,* Tato Morales, 2023, https://cestlis.bandcamp.com/album/empires.

194   *Above all, trust:* Pierre Teilhard de Chardin, "Patient Trust," published in Nancy L. Bieber, *Decision Making and Spiritual Discernment: The Sacred Art of Finding Your Way* (Woodstock, VT: SkyLight Paths, 2010), 156-57.

About the Author

JODI H. GRUBBS is a wife, mom, friend, and slow-living guide. She is the host of the podcast *Our Island in the City*, where she and her guests discuss aspects of slower living, soul care, and deep community. Through her writing and podcasting, Jodi gives others permission to slow down to be present in their right-now lives. She can often be found enjoying coffee and conversation with a friend at her local coffee shop. She lives in a 1950s bungalow on the outskirts of Raleigh, North Carolina. Follow Jodi at jodigrubbs.com or on Instagram at jodi.grubbs for your own gentle invitation to exhale.

Like this book?
Scan the code to discover more content like this!

Get on IVP's email list to receive special offers, exclusive book news, and thoughtful content from your favorite authors on topics you care about.

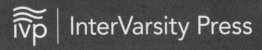
InterVarsity Press